RELIGIOUS
WOMAN

DENISE LARDNER CARMODY

~

RELIGIOUS WOMAN

~

Contemporary Reflections on Eastern Texts

CROSSROAD • NEW YORK

291.17834
Car

1991

The Crossroad Publishing Company
370 Lexington Avenue, New York, NY 10017

Copyright © 1991 by Denise Lardner Carmody

All rights reserved. No part of this book may be reproduced, stored in
a retrieval system, or transmitted, in any form or by any means,
electronic, mechanical, photocopying, recording, or otherwise, without
the written permission of The Crossroad Publishing Company.

Printed in the United States of America
Typesetting output: TEXSource, Houston

Library of Congress Cataloging-in-Publication Data

Carmody, Denise Lardner, 1935–
    Religious woman: contemporary reflections on Eastern texts /
Denise Lardner Carmody.
        p. cm.
    ISBN 0-8245-1065-8
    1. Women and religion. 2. Women—Religious life. I. Title.
BL458.C36 1991
291.1'78344—dc20   90-43276
                                                             CIP

For Marion Kirk

Contents

Preface

This book is a companion or complement to my previous *Biblical Woman* (Crossroad, 1988). As with that book, I provide here both historical context and contemporary reflection. The texts that I have chosen should enable readers to begin a serious dialogue with the Eastern traditions. By engaging with Islamic, Hindu, Buddhist, Chinese, and Japanese texts bearing on women, readers should find themselves pondering again the mysteries of sexual complementarity and antagonism.

On the whole, the Eastern story is not uplifting. While all the traditions have found reasons to respect women, all have also subordinated women to men and given women a lesser share in what they finally considered most valuable. Nonetheless, Eastern women have survived, and I find it more useful to ponder their strengths than to lament their sufferings. As well, I think that the overall message of this book is encouraging. The raw material for friendship and equality between the sexes is as readily available in Eastern texts as in Western biblical ones.

My thanks to Frank Oveis, my editor at Crossroad, for sponsoring this project; to my husband, John Carmody, for helpful reactions; to the students in courses on women and world religions who have helped me to sharpen my perceptions; and to Marion Kirk, who for twenty years has been a shining example of intelligence, courage, and faith.

Introduction
Religious Woman

During the nineteenth century American women gained the reputation of being the more religious sex. Whereas men had the charge to deal with the sooty outside world, women were to tend to the home and family. Whereas men dealt with harsh realities — warfare, business, government — women were to nurture the finer, spiritual things. Among these were what were considered religious sentiments (though often they were as much aesthetic): sensitivity to natural beauty, compassion for suffering humanity, attunement to delicacy of feeling, sweetness, and tranquility of spirit.

That is not the sense of femininity or religion that interests me in this book. The horizon against which I want to set these reflections is the millennial story of humanity's struggle to accommodate itself to the mysteriousness of its world, its condition. My assumption, for which it would not be difficult to bring forward evidence, is that men and women have shared equally in this mysterious human condition. Whatever the differences in tasks and roles their cultures set them, men and women the world over have been amazed at newborn life, troubled at careless death, brought ecstatically alive by marvelous sunsets, had their spirits crushed by heartless cruelty. When they have experienced genuine love, they have felt that whoever or whatever was responsible for their condition was surpassingly good. When they have experienced genuine hate, they have worried that the world was diabolical. Neither sex has had an advantage or an exemption in these matters. Both sexes have known, from common sense and education alike, that their fates are radically similar.

11

Whatever the value their culture has placed on their sex-specified roles and images, through the ages women and men have also known that they need one another. To have offspring and realize anything like the fullness of human potential, the sexes could not dwell apart in segregation. They had to interact at numerous levels. This interaction was the source of much of their joy and excitement, as well as of much of their sharpest pain. But, for better or worse, richer or poorer, they were welded together, bound to work out a common destiny.

This fundamental fact has shaped the religion (the dealings with ultimate mysteriousness) of women in all cultures. Paleolithic women, whose fertility could make them the primary analogues of the Great Mother who was their tribe's first image of divinity, lived in a world of wonders that included male power, intelligence, skill, and sexual functions. Women of recent oral cultures like the Native American knew that their power to bring forth new life stood in a dialectical relationship with men's power to kill game and enemies. The women whose cultures owed much to biblical revelation reverenced ancestors such as Sarah and Mary, who played capital roles in a story of salvation (a narrative unfolding of how divinity might be healing all people). Muslim women reverenced Khadija and Fatima, the wife and daughter of Muhammad, considering them exemplary "submitters" to the Allah who wanted all heads to bow. In the Middle East, Europe, North America, Latin America, and other lands where Jewish, Christian, and Muslim imagery flourished, women were as much called to salvation, as much included in the basic narrative, as men.

Certainly, one has to say that men have dominated the institutional aspects of virtually all the world's cultures. But saying that does not make religion exclusive to either women or men. Prior to the nineteenth century (for our American cultural history), religion was so pervasive a part of the world's cultures that it absorbed women and men equally.

There are signs that a postmodern culture now aborning may restore some of the integrity that nineteenth- and twentieth-century secularism has forfeited. There are signs that the physical and the spiritual, the bodily and the mental, what we consign to nature and what we consign to culture, may all become less dichotomous. Both sexes have suffered from the mechanism favored by modernity, and both have much to gain from the more organic models for cultural health now proposed on every side. If women are credited with a traditionally stronger instinct for such holism, that does not mean that many men don't long for a better marriage between mind and heart, intellect and feeling. If men are charged with a traditionally stronger blindness to the vulnerabilities of nature and the costs of aggression, that does not mean that many women have not been guilty of supporting them and replicating their mistakes.

The times are ripe for reflections on religion and women's experience that nourish both sexes' renewed appreciation of the mysteriousness of the human condition. Arguably, our species' health — physical, mental, and cultural alike — depends on our coming to terms with both how much we do not know and how nourishing the contemplation of divine mystery can be. When we accept that we do not understand the most basic facts about our human condition — where we came from, where we are going, why we have to die, why goodness is so fragile, why evil is so potent, how and why love arises, what makes people creative — we can enter upon a great liberation. When we contemplate our existence so that we enter a cloud of unknowing (an overshadowing of the analytical mind) that allows us to embrace the totality of Being in simple love, we can often experience a great healing. By assuring us that we are part of something not only much greater but also much more personal than ourselves, the contemplation that is at the heart of the world's religious experience allows us to accept and feel good about what we cannot understand. It allows us to live by faith, hope, and charity, those primary strengths vital to a sense of grace.

And what is a sense of grace? For our purposes here, it is the perception, by feeling and imagination and intelligence conjoined, that the mysteriousness of our human condition is wonderful — much better than we have any right to expect. When felt to be graced, the human condition has limitless possibilities.

Indeed, they stretch far beyond the grave, reaching right into the nature of the creative power and love that we intuit must be responsible for the universe.

This is the way I want to think about the religion that women have shared equally with men throughout the ages: mystagogically (as an activation of our human senses of wonder and honesty, in face of the infinity of the reality we contemplate in our best human moments). But I also want to imply that this religion has been marvelously diverse and concrete. The beads of Indian dancers, the mulled wine of European revelers, the face-scarrings of African warriors, the ululations of Middle Eastern women, the worn Bibles of American Puritans, the robes of Eastern Orthodox priests, the dances of Hasidic Jews, the chants of Buddhist monks — all have played a part in the display of human religiosity. All have made an impact, great or small, on the senses, imaginations, minds, and hearts of the women and men who have lived within their cultural ambit. If the core of the human condition being probed and celebrated was everywhere a fathomless, incomprehensible mystery, the cultural "clothing" was precise, detailed, and idiosyncratic. Mexican women were religious differently from German women. Iranian women wore clothing different from Japanese women and served their families different food. Yet traditional Mexican, German, Iranian, and Japanese women all lived in cultures that considered clothing and food religiously significant. All lived in cultures that were holistic and so could find appearing in any cultural particular the mysteriousness that riveted its soul. The outcroppings of religion — response to ultimate mystery — have been as various as the ecological niches and individual creativities of both regional cultures and particular people. The One of the ultimate mysteriousness of the human condition has illumined the vast many of humanity's cultural creations. So the religious woman who draws my mind's eye here has been just a female representative of *homo religiosus*: humanity at its richest, in face of ultimate mystery.[1]

Contemporary Reflections on Eastern Texts

Several years ago I published a book of contemporary reflections on the experiences of women suggested by the Bible.[2] Now I am undertaking something parallel for the experiences of women suggested by Eastern sacred texts. Here "Eastern" means Muslim, Hindu, Buddhist, Chinese, and Japanese. In each case, I hope to suggest both how their religious culture led the women in question to think about themselves and how present-day American women might most profitably think about such Eastern problems or insights. The structure of this book is therefore dialogical. We move from the sense of religion suggested in the prior section to Eastern religious texts bearing on women. Then we move from those texts back to present-day American culture. The result should be an ongoing conversation between the present and the past, between Western assumptions and Eastern assumptions.

To present the likely experience of Eastern women sympathetically, it is necessary to situate the texts we are using in their historical and philosophical contexts. Thus, the first concern in each section will be to explain what the text in question probably meant on its own terms. Following such an explanation, we can ask the further question, What can this text offer us today? This further question is speculative. It stimulates images of how we think about women and men nowadays, as well as images of how we think about ultimate reality — divine mystery. If we take such a stimulus to heart, we may find that the women suggested by the Eastern texts are indeed our sisters. Whether we are females or males, we may find that their struggles to become fully human by dealing with what their culture taught them about themselves and how to relate to ultimate reality are much like our own.

In saying this I am assuming that we present-day Americans are the equals of prior peoples in other lands when it comes to the basic task of finding meaning in a mysterious world. Religion, understood as efforts to fulfill this task, is a great leveler. As well, it is a great nourishment for all the people who find contemplating their human condition fascinating. Because such a contemplation is not well known in contemporary American culture, it may be useful to conclude this Introduction by reflecting on religious contemplation.

"Handsome is as handsome does" is a representative American proverb. We Americans continue to be a pragmatic people. We tend to judge projects, ideas, and even individual human beings by results. I find that this judgment can be both wise and superficial. It is wise when it expresses the insight that action is the fullest language in which human beings express themselves. What people say is not so significant as what they do. How people actually spend their money, spend their time, respond to crises, treat their spouses and children day in and day out gives us the best clue to their values, their humanity. So, when pragmatism expresses the priority of action or praxis over promises, it expresses considerable wisdom.

On the other hand, pragmatism can degenerate into a superficial view of projects, ideas, and people. It can take the form of the accountant's "bottom line," which ignores any but financial criteria of success. Equally, pragmatists can fall in line behind the pundits of the media, who have short memories and a great love of glitter. When they do, they tend to judge projects, people, and ideas by woefully inadequate criteria: popularity polls, access to supposed circles of power, frequency of appearance on the society pages. Forgetting the dubious character of all these standards, many judges of popular culture reduce the human venture to the point of caricature. Having no appreciation for profound creativity or endurance in the realms of art, science, statecraft, philosophy, or religion, they ignore what makes the human species most human.

A less pragmatic, more contemplative view of the human spirit is interested in being as well as doing. While admiring the insight that what people do with their time and money is a good index of their values, contemplative judges are more interested in how people situate themselves in the world. Specifically, they are more interested in how people grapple with the great questions of death and life, of goodness and evil, of creativity and barrenness. of superficiality and depth. Contemplation helps people realize the paradoxical quality of human meaning. Socrates going to his death was more fully alive than the people who had condemned him. Jesus hanging on the cross was the personification of defeat yet from his death came a great resurrection of human hopes. The Buddha who had no desire for worldly goods or honors was the richest person in India. The humble mystic Rabi'a who loved Allah selflessly gained a fulfillment few princes ever found.

Where does this paradoxical quality of human existence come from? From our contemplative perception that the mysteriousness of our condition throws all our spontaneous assumptions into question. If we do not know, with the sort of empirical certainty we want, where we have come from and where we are going, we cannot be sure that what we have chosen to live for is fully wise. We always have to wonder whether there isn't a different, better scale of values, a more wondrous treasure on which to set our hearts. Regularly, people who think about this matter have to question the value of possessions. Regularly, the monks and nuns who set out to be full-time contemplatives choose a simple, stripped lifestyle. Possessions can be great distractions. Responsibilities can choke the spirit. Family life, business, politics, and even religious services can all come to taste like straw. If the one thing necessary is to gain harmony with the divine mystery, to please one's God, then most of what preoccupies most people is trivial.

However, this judgment in turn can come under attack. In the series of Zen teaching pictures known as "herding an ox" we find that the last stages of enlightenment take people back into the world. When their enlightenment is mature, they can find harmony everywhere. As well, they can make their compassion for other people practical by living in other people's midst, as examples, teachers, helpers. Jews, Christians, and Muslims have made the same argument. Judaism has frowned on monasticism, thinking that family life is the better context for serving God and gaining wisdom. Christianity has worshiped an incarnate divinity who lived in the world, first earning his bread as a carpenter and then consorting with common people, to teach and cure them. Islam has looked to Muhammad as its great model, stressing that Muhammad enjoyed the closest communion with God while at the head of a large family, a growing religious community, and even armies fighting for Allah.

So there is paradox upon paradox when a culture honors contemplation. Language and narrative both tend to become metaphorical, because reality itself becomes richer than what one can render in exact, denotational terms. Reality has several levels, endless interconnections, a central incomprehensibility. What does the copula "is" signify? Why "is" there something rather than nothing? How can the human mind, obviously a faculty of a mortal, finite being, map galaxies whose numbers and ages approach infinity? And always there is the pressure not only to comprehend, and so control, the reality in which one is immersed but also to love it. Always, the deepest desire of the human spirit is to unite itself with the divine mystery and so become holy, mighty, and immortal like its God.

Without neglecting what our texts tell us about the physical circumstances in the lives of Eastern women, our focus will fall more sharply on the contemplative possibilities that the texts suggest. In other words, what in these documents that have had a great influence on our Eastern sisters, and brothers, might stir us to greater wisdom today? That is my major interest, and I hope that I can present these Eastern texts with enough wit to draw readers into it.

1
Islamic Texts

They will question thee concerning the monthly course. Say: "It is hurt; so go apart from women during the monthly course, and do not approach them till they are clean."[1]

—Qur'an 2:222

The Qur'an is the most important book in Islam. Indeed, it is the most important resource of Islam, the great center. Islam thinks of itself as the genuine religion that all people ought to offer Allah (God). To raise up this genuine religion, Allah sent various prophets: Abraham, Moses, Jesus, and others. People kept backsliding into idolatry, however, so Allah made a definitive revelation through Muhammad. The Qur'an is that revelation. It gathers together the materials that Allah commanded Muhammad to proclaim. Of itself, the Qur'an is eternal. Many Muslims think of it as always having existed alongside Allah. Strictly speaking, one cannot translate it from Arabic. In all ways it takes priority in Islam as the best indication of the divine will.

The Arab society to which Muhammad (570–632) was preaching early in the seventh century was patriarchal. Women had circumscribed roles and did not lead clans. On the other hand, women could become wealthy, as Muhammad's first wife, Khadija, had become, and women exercised considerable informal influence on men. The great task of women, however, was to conceive, bear, and raise children. Muhammad improved the condition of women, gave them many legal rights, and limited Muslim men to four wives (monogamy has been the Islamic ideal). Still, the men who have ruled Islam have usually interpreted the

19

Qur'anic texts bearing on women in a patriarchal fashion, so that women have usually been considered the dependents of their fathers, husbands, or elder sons.

This text on menstruation suggests the complex reaction to women that Muslim men were expected to have. First, despite the naturalness of menstruation, men (the Qur'an tends to assume that its primary audience is male) are to consider it like a wound. Something is injured, not quite right. So, second, men are to stay apart from women during menstruation. Most importantly, they are to refrain from sexual intercourse, but the text also suggests a broader withdrawal. Thus it has seemed good for Muslim women to seclude themselves during menstruation.

Third, the Qur'an explicitly equates menstruation with uncleanness. This is a notion that many cultures have shared. Natural though it be, menstruation renders women unfit for contact. Usually this contact has ritualistic overtones. Until they have ceased menstruating and purified themselves, women should not participate in public worship. Scholars sometimes call this attitude a "blood taboo." As such, it can apply not only to menstruating women but also to women who have just given birth, to warriors who have slain another human being, and to people who have had contact with the dead. Blood stands for life itself, so the shedding of blood has seemed to many peoples awesome, frightening, and dangerous. The "uncleanness" associated with menstruation or contact with the dead is therefore less physical than emotional. It has a physical basis, but the main force it carries is something that upsets people's sense of what is whole and so able to associate with the holy.

Fourth, it is possible to find in this verse a tender concern for women. Hurt, vulnerable, women could elicit from men an instinct to take care of them, or at least not to burden them further. The history of how Islamic men have treated women might not support the thesis that such a tender concern has prevailed, but the text provides the possibility and there is no reason to think that Muslim men who loved their mothers, wives, and daughters did not realize it sometimes.

When one considers this text against the backdrop of Islam as a whole and then thinks about the current situation of American women, what stands out is the strangeness, the otherness, that men and women have found in one another so regularly. Because most of the canonical texts have been written by men and have had men in mind as their primary audience, women tend to appear as the strange or deviant sex, but it could have been otherwise. Had women been the primary authors or audience, we might find that men would appear strange or deviant and so call forth peculiar commentaries.

Obviously, the question of how the sexes perceive one another and relate is complicated beyond compare. Sexual roles go to the heart of family life and wider culture, shaping and being shaped by everything that human beings think and do. Yet it is remarkable how much otherness the two sexes continue to find in one another. Generation after generation, the humanity they share is both obscured and enriched by their perception that the other sex may be as unlike as like them. Inasmuch as men dominate a given culture's institutions, this tends to work out so that women's ways seem the less comprehensible and the more to be feared. On the other hand, women bond together by affirming their own ways and wondering about the strangeness of the ways of men.

An image from the end of the football season comes to mind. Down on the field the star quarterback is running for his life. He is goodly sized, but after him are two three-hundred pound behemoths. In the stands his attractive wife, fey in a bolero hat, bows her head and covers her eyes. He scampers free and completes a key pass. She looks completely drained. It is a strange ritual. On the one hand, perhaps a third of the people in the stands are women, cheering their lungs out. The men who play the game, and the men who toast it so lustily, raising their cans of beer, seem to like to have their women around. On the other hand, the women appear both thrilled and appalled. They get caught up into the crowd's lust for victory, yet they wince at each savage tackle. A few of them are probably genuine fans, but many more would probably say, in private moments, that the whole thing is very strange. Risking ruined knees for the rest of one's life in order to advance a leather oval across a line of chalk — what in the world drives these guys?

It does not take a grand extrapolation to move from football to the machismo of war and other less benign forms of combat. The play of men runs along the edge of violence so frequently that it has to give women pause. Certainly, women can have their modes of violence, not the least being their support of wars. But the lines that Mary Morris quotes at the beginning of her fine novel *The Waiting Room* suggest that women seldom understand war: "We are the only ones who are still waiting, in a suspense as old as time, that of women, everywhere, waiting for the men to come home from the war."[2]

The Qur'an, which in places becomes quite martial, talking about the need to battle infidels, might suggest that women are not warlike because they are wounded by nature. For that line of thought, women would know in their bodies the vulnerability of human flesh — how easily it can bleed — and also the mystery of the ties among blood, death, and new life. That is a sort of reflection that raises enormous problems for feminists, because it has been used so regularly to marginalize women, yet it remains intriguing. Indeed, it is not hard to turn it to feminist account: women should have a special say when it comes to warfare and violence, because they have a special perception of what shedding blood implies and costs.

However one evaluates this line of thought, it can remind us that genuine religion ought to be a reconciler of women and men. In the perspective of ultimate, divine mystery, the games that human beings play, and the wars by which they slaughter one another, brim with paradox. Who is the victor and who the victim, when people go to war? What are the profits, and what the losses, when a violent game becomes a national pastime? Is the quarterback scampering to safety a hero, or is he another macho fool? Is his wife in the stands, shielding her eyes, a privileged interpreter of such matters, or does her sex render her unable to understand?

~ ~ ~

Men are the managers of the affairs of women for that God has preferred in bounty one of them over another, and for that they

*have expended of their property. Righteous women are therefore
obedient....*

—Qur'an 4:38

In the Qur'an, men are in control and women are subservient.
That is simply the way that God has ordered the human condition. Women's affairs — their property, their children, and the
overall disposition of their lives — are not autonomous. They
come under the authority and oversight of fathers, husbands, and
elder sons. Throughout her life cycle, the Muslim woman idealized by the Qur'an obeys the men set over her. In obeying them,
she is obeying Allah. Indeed, in popular Muslim lore the main
reason that some women languish in the Fire (hell) and do not
make it to the Garden (heaven) is that they have disobeyed their
husbands.[3]

It bears noting that this divine providence ties into the social fact that men regularly spend money on women. Women
cost men, in various ways, and that cost justifies men's rule over
women. Whether the Qur'an has in mind the bride-price that
could be exacted or the outlay that a family was bound to require, it assumes that men are the main providers. From this
assumption, it follows that men are the overlords: spending justifies control.

If we try to bring a sympathetic imagination to the origins
of Islam, when the Qur'an was transforming the clan culture
of traditional Arabia, we may picture a situation in which men
have to purchase women and then provide for them, if the men
are to establish households and beget progeny. A man who pur-
chased a camel expected to control it, to use it as he saw fit.
Without equating a woman with a camel, we can see how the
logic linking acquisition to control could make men the rulers
of women. To be sure, the Qur'an gives women rights against
abuse, and the best of the traditional Muslim lawyers interpreted
such rights generously. Nonetheless, this text is akin to certain
biblical texts (for example, Colossians 3:18, 1 Timothy 2:11) in
making men the superiors and women the obedient underlings.
No properly benevolent reading of the text, according to which
men are counseled to generosity, or even to love, can take away

the suggestion that in the basic nature of things men should be in charge. (For Muslim folklore, one of the signs of the end of history is a reversal of this order. When women rule, the Judgment Day is nigh.) What ought we to make of this attitude, which has prevailed in most cultures throughout history and caused the majority of women to feel that their lives were out of their hands?

If we are not to be anachronistic, we have to realize that premodern cultures thought that creation had natural laws, and that for many such cultures one such natural law was the priority of men over women. Order ultimately went back to what the Creator had encoded in creation, and the order passed down as tribal wisdom was that men should rule and women obey. On the other hand, if we are not to be naive, we have to realize that this general outlook admitted many different applications. Women could become expert in getting men to "rule" as the women wished. Women could play one game in the presence of men and another when left to themselves. "Obeying" could be servile, or generous, or pro forma, or mocking. Women have always had as much wit as men, so women's fulfillments of their stipulated roles have been as various as men's fulfillments of male roles.

Still, what strikes me now is the duplicity, in the sense of "doubleness," that assumptions such as this one of the Qur'an have introduced into women's consciousness. Studying contemporary American girls, the developmental psychologist Carol Gilligan and her associates have found that whereas many eleven-year-olds have a clear sense of themselves and the world, most sixteen-year-olds are confused. When asked to explain this unfortunate changeover, Gilligan has to suggest that the girls come to realize that most of their culture is stacked against them, in the sense that it assumes that women are marginal to mainstream social power and that women's voice is second to men's. Thus the girls tend to lose confidence and become tentative. As their bodies mature and they move into interactions with males that are emotionally more significant, their lives become terribly complicated.[4]

For some women, this complication eventually produces a sophistication about social reality so rich as partially to redeem it. For many others, the price of living with the awareness that one will always be a member of the second, less authoritative and less valued sex is so high that it goes unredeemed. Self-doubt, crippling creativity, joy, and even faith, occurs so regularly that pride is seldom women's capital sin. More frequently, women sin by cowardice — lacking the courage to be.

Even this assessment is too harsh, however, because one has to ask how much freedom most women have had. When their culture has broadcast day and night that, if they are righteous, they obey the men in their lives, it is not surprising that many find little will to assert themselves.

Once again, we have to resist stereotypes and remind ourselves that a great many women have asserted themselves, in small ways and great. As though knowing in their bones that something was awry, and feeling bound as a matter of conscience to honor this feeling, they have burned their husbands' eggs, or gotten the vapors, or developed colossal tempers, or become possessed by jinn (the spirits that Islam has often allowed women to follow). Society needs safety valves. It cannot allow the tensions between men and women to stay red-hot, lest there be so many explosions that normal life be impossible. So, indirectly, obliquely, many cultures sanction women's flightiness, or self-indulgence, or religiosity, or other somewhat exceptional behavior, as ways that women may escape a heavy-handed interpretation of men's divine right to rule. The steel magnolia of southern American cultural stereotype is an example of such accommodation. When Rumpole of the Bailey sighs and bows to "She who must be obeyed," we enjoy a British example. Indeed, all of the cultures that have defined the domestic zone as women's sphere, with the implication that men should keep their hands off, have been acknowledging the injustice of excluding women from sharing power in the wider, public sphere.

Contemplating this now tragic, now comic pattern among the sexes the world over, one might wonder how much it matters in the long run that women have generally been the wards of men. The question is impossible to answer, of course, but enough malignant data exist to make one think that bringing women to official, culturally fully accepted, equality with men is very important. First, there is the matter of the equanimity and proper self-esteem of half of the human race. Because this is a psychological matter, rather than a matter of economics or warfare (upon which it impinges, of course), does not mean that we should dismiss it as trivial. Cultures exist only to make life bearable and beautiful for the people who inhabit them. If half the population is crippled by cultural images and stereotypes, the culture in question needs drastic revision.

Second, inadequate, distorting stipulations of the relations between the sexes warp a culture through and through. There is, objectively, a radical equality between the sexes that a culture denies or fails to incarnate and institutionalize only at its peril. Women know as much about death and life, truth and lies, divinity and humanity, love and hate, as men. These are the mainsprings of the human condition. Women share them with men as full equals. Not to provide for this in laws and mores is to fly in the face of a crucial reality. Women are as intelligent, as virtuous, as flawed, as troubled — in a word as human — as men. When men pretend that they should control women's destiny, saying that God has decreed this, or that their financial support of women justifies it, or that their greater physical strength makes it their right, they sin against the light. Clearly, such sinning against the light has reached into the inner precincts of many religious groups. The Roman Curia that tries to control how Catholics think, the religious councils that rule Iran, the leaders of many Hasidic Jewish sects, and many leading Hindu gurus are all guilty of sinning against the manifest equality of women in humanity. What this says about divine mystery is an interesting question. Most likely it says that on Judgment Day the motherly God will embarrass many religious leaders.

~ ~ ~

Whosoever does evil shall be recompensed for it, and will not find for him, apart from God, a friend or helper. And whosoever does deeds of righteousness, be it male or female, believing — they shall enter paradise....

—Qur'an 4:123

Here we have a Qur'anic text affirming the basic equality of men
and women before God. When it comes to final destiny, how people have behaved will be the major criterion. Ethically, men and
women stand on an equal footing. Each sex will be judged by its
deeds, be they evil or righteous. If a man does righteous deeds, in
faith that such are Allah's will, he will enter Paradise. If a woman
does righteous deeds, in faith that such are Allah's will, she will
also enter Paradise. So sex finally matters less than righteousness.
To enjoy God in the fulfillment for which the human being has
been made, it does not matter whether one is male or female. It
matters only that one has done what God required.

And what does the Qur'an assume that God requires? In the
first place, that people confess that God is one. The capital ar-
ticle in the Muslim creed is, "There is no God but God, and
Muhammad is his Prophet." The quintessence of righteousness
is to be a believer in this only God. The quintessence of evil is to
fail to believe and so be an idolater. To set anything in the place
of Allah is to ruin human nature, both in time and for eternity.
Everything falls into disorder, becomes disjointed, when God is
not the sole Lord.

Commentators regularly make the point that this vigorous
Muslim monotheism drew strength from two sources. It affirmed
the monotheism of the Bible, and it rejected the polytheism of
pre-Muslim Arab culture. Muslims believe that the revelations to
Muhammad were much more than an updating of the revelations
held by Jews and Christians, but they consider Jews and Christians to worship the same single God who made Muhammad his
definitive spokesman ("the seal of the prophets"). Christians have
erred seriously, however, by teaching that God is a trinity (as well
as a unity), and by believing that Jesus was divine. In Muslim perspective, nothing can share divinity with Allah. Allah has no need
to be a community, and no creature could partake of the divine
nature. So, God can have no "Son," as Christians proclaim.

The uniqueness of Allah leads to his sole lordship. He has no
competitors for the allegiance of the good Muslim. The "space"
between God and the believer should be empty of any inter-
mediate deities. God directly controls all things in nature and all
human fates. Still, Islam believes in angels, and it has accorded

both Muhammad and the Qur'an the status of holy intermediaries
between human beings and Allah. Muhammad emphatically is
not divine. He is completely human, and so Muslim faith in
him is different from Christian faith in Jesus. Islam honors Jesus,
accepting the story of his virgin birth, but it rejects the strong
version of Jesus's prophecy that makes him the Word of God
incarnate. As a prophet, Jesus was preparatory and inferior to
Muhammad.

In Islam, the closest thing to the Word of God incarnate is the
Qur'an. As mentioned, for many Muslims the Qur'an is eternal.
The majority of Muslims probably still consider God the author
of the Qur'an in the literal sense that God spoke the words one
now finds on the pages. The many problems that the modern,
critical mind finds with a fundamentalism of this sort strike conservative Muslims as signs of unbelief. Inasmuch as such a critical
mind has become dominant in the West, it shows the degeneracy
of the Western cultures.

Insofar as they are held to the same standards as men when
it comes to entering Paradise, women are as involved with these
fundamentals of Muslim faith as men. What women have to believe, as the basis of their righteous deeds, is just what men have
to believe. For faithful Muslim women, there is no Allah but Allah and Muhammad is his Prophet. Indeed, for faithful Muslim
women this is the stuff of lullabies to their children, the best
thing to croon.[5]

Now, if we ask about a contemporary American appreciation
of this Muslim data on the radical equality of men and women
and on the radical faith that both have to muster if they are to
enter Paradise, some interesting reflections arise. For example, we
realize that a culture can deal with its intuitions of women's full
humanity before God in either of two divergent ways. It can say
that equality before God is the most important thing, that the
most important thing ought to rule cultural roles and images,
and so that men and women should be equal before the law, in
work, in parenting, in access to religious authority, in the councils
that run the tribe, village, or nation. Only a few groups, such as
the Shakers, have taken this route.

The other route amounts to a religious patriarchalism that

usually wants to be benign. Granting that the sexes are equal when it comes to their final destiny, and making their final destiny all-important, those following this second route claim that civic, cultural, historical matters are relatively unimportant and so need not try to replicate the equality that men and women have before God on Judgment Day. In other words, it doesn't matter that men rule over women, or that women come up short by such secular indices as money, power, education, respect, and the like. All of the arrangements that cultures create are provisional and passing. Therefore those given rule should not exult and those asked to obey should not sulk.

In most religious cultures neither of these two options is so clear, however, because usually the major mores are said to have been dictated by God. So while women and men may be equal on Judgment Day, divine wisdom has decreed that before Judgment Day men should take priority. It is not a matter of indifference, because God has decreed this priority of men. But if pushed to explain the apparent injustice of such a decree, most defenders of patriarchy resort to either a crude fideism (one must simply accept that that's the way the Qur'an or the Bible lays it out) or a depreciation of the ultimate significance of any inequality: life is short and Paradise is long.

Faced with the shifts, the slipperiness, of such defenses of patriarchy, thoughtful women realize that the game is not about truth, consistency, or justice, but about power. Again and again, male religious establishments assert women's ultimate equality with men, in order to hold women to the rigorous standards necessary for pleasing God. Equally regularly, however, those authorities refuse to grant women cultural equality. So thoughtful women conclude that men want to control women's consciences but not be subject to any counter-controls from women, even those generated by the competition in sanctity or social service that the cultural equality of women could generate. It is more important that men rule than that justice or logic or truly religious criteria (for example, that authority should flow from demonstrable wisdom and sanctity) should prevail.

This makes many women cynical about religious institutions, as about all of the institutions that men rule. Interestingly, though, it can also make women more religious than men. Because it was clear that they would receive no justice from human institutions, most of which were dominated by men, myriad women have placed their hopes in God. Not being limited and flawed like human beings, God could and would see wronged women done right. God could and would wipe every tear from their eyes, and injustice would be no more. While this attitude had obvious dangers, most religious women were so involved in issues of basic survival — food, clothing, shelter, child-rearing, elementary education, nursing — that there was little danger they would not keep their feet on the ground. If their hearts found rest in contemplating heaven, who could fault them? Thus, whether most Muslim teachers realized it or not, verses such as this one from the Qur'an liberated many women, and some men, from the tyrannies of patriarchy. Simply by making women and men equal on Judgment Day, a verse such as this gave people suffering injustice a profound reason to hope that one day all would be made right.

~ ~ ~

O Prophet, say to thy wives and daughters and the believing women, that they draw their veils close to them; so it is likelier they will be known, and not hurt. God is All-forgiving, All-compassionate.

—Qur'an 33:59

The traditional Muslim practice of veiling women derives from this and similar passages in the Qur'an. In other texts, the rationale is more pernicious: women are to veil what might incite men to lust. Here the rationale keeps lust at some remove: by veiling themselves, believing women symbolize their faith (and purity), making known (to men of good will) who they are (women not loose and available for men's free use).

With the resurgence of traditional Muslim cultures in many countries, the practice of veiling women has returned. For example, it became a major symbol in the restoration of a Muslim regime in Iran, so that women courted serious punishments if they went unveiled. In the early decades of the twentieth century, when some Muslim countries sought to modernize themselves by Western standards, putting aside the veil was a woman's rite of passage to emancipation. The reasons why present-day Muslim women resume wearing the veil can be many, but prominent among them are a genuine desire to embrace traditional Islamic standards and a weariness with the harassment of men, whether sexual or religious.[6]

In addition to legislating that women go about veiled, some Muslim countries created *purdah* — women's wholesale seclusion from public life. Among the ruling and wealthy classes, *purdah* could also mean living in a harem. Since men were allowed up to four wives, as long as they could provide for them financially and emotionally, wealthy Muslim men sometimes ran polygynous households. The rulers who had dozens of consorts violated both the letter and spirit of the Qur'an, but in some ways their harems merely extended the logic of polygynous households. Wives and consorts were to be secluded from public life, so that they might not tempt men who had no right to them and so that they might not disgrace their husbands. Analogously, daughters, nieces, and other female members of a man's household were held to veiling and seclusion in order to safeguard his honor.

Several commentators have noted that when traditionalists sought to stave off the inrush of modern, Western cultural values, they instinctively rushed to defend what they considered the purity of their women. They might concede that politics, business, and education could profit from exposure to Western progress, but they tended to be adamant that their women should not follow Western models of emancipation. On the one hand, they could argue effectively that Western cultures were often awash in divorce, the breakdown of family life, and promiscuity (pornography, prostitution, venereal disease). On the other hand, Muslim cultures were not without their parallel problems, and if one judges men's control of women's potential a significant social problem, many Muslim lands cried out for reform. So veiling, as a sign of the past, a symbol of the traditional way of regarding Muslim women as separated from the corruptions of public life, could become a matter of raging debate.

I am more interested in the issue of women's supposed danger to men, and so seclusion from public life, than in the pros and cons of traditional Muslim (or modern Western) sexual mores. What strikes me, and no doubt most other feminists, is the ego-centricity of the judgment that the first significance of women's clothing is its impact on men. As soon as one admits that judgment, the cause of sexual equality has been lost. For that judgment makes men the pivot of culture and devastates any assumption that the two sexes share humanity equally. If they did share humanity equally, the way that women dress would be no more and no less significant than the way that men dress.

Is this argument naive, overlooking or paying little attention to the typical pattern of sexual arousal, according to which men are first attracted to women by physical beauty and so women try to make themselves alluring? That is an interesting question. What is naiveté? Should we label naive a view that understands how many people regard the attractions between the sexes but thinks that such a regard is superficial, compared to the matters that religious contemplation finds truly significant? Anyone with eyes and a brain knows that dress is a factor in sexual attraction. The advertising media make a living off this fact, selling everything from cars to television sets by using sexy women. But anyone with a soul, a spiritual center capable of absorption with divine mystery, knows that the fashion and advertising industries are at best irrelevant and at worst enemies of a truly significant human existence. Ironically, by placing such emphasis on women's veiling, Islam has sometimes become more like the fashion and advertising industries than like the friends of a truly significant human existence.

Why should women bear the major responsibility for what misfires between the sexes? Why is there not an even-handed approach, so that women dress sensibly and men think of women as more than objects of sexual pleasure? Indeed, why do so many religions remain prudish, unable to accept the goodness of sexuality and so the fun, the sport, of healthy seduction? It is amazing that religions supposedly convinced of the goodness of creation make an exception when it comes to practical provisions for sexual attraction. Virtually all of the great world religions — Judaism, Christianity, Islam, Hinduism, Buddhism, Confucianism, Taoism, Shinto — offer many reasons for marveling at the goodness of creation. Yet these same religions have also tolerated, or even encouraged, prudishness about sex. No doubt the religions house other significant contradictions, but this one stands out the world over. And wherever it does stand out, women bear the brunt of the pain that results.

Consider, for example, the dreadful phenomenon of female circumcision (clitoridectomy and infibulation). Africa is the great basin of this practice, and Islam has often tolerated it. The usual rationale offered for female circumcision is that it safeguards the chastity of girls and makes them desirable wives. Manifestly, 90 percent of this perception comes from men's minds. Granted, grandmothers and mothers who have been circumcised exert great pressure on young girls to follow suit, either because they believe the practice has been beneficial or because they want the next generation to suffer as they had to. Still, I find it impossible to believe that, left to themselves, women would sponsor such mutilation.

For, of course, that is exactly what it is. Female circumcision greatly reduces the girl's ability to experience sexual pleasure, and in many cases it causes serious, even mortal, infection.[7] God alone knows what it does to girls' psyches and how it shapes their conjugal lives. The Qur'an does not advocate female circumcision, and one can argue that it should oppose the practice as a denigration of Allah's creation. But in its texts on veiling the Qur'an does open the door to the sort of reasoning that African Muslims tend to use to justify female circumcision. If women are temptresses, or cannot be trusted to control their sexual desires, and if sexual transgression is an especially serious offense against Allah (something that requires more proof than what one usually receives), then it makes sense to take stern measures to control women's sexuality. Draping women in concealing clothing is one step, but it may not prove sufficient. The final stage in this line of thought, which I consider the *reductio ad absurdum*, is female circumcision. In order to safeguard men's souls, one slashes the organic basis of women's sexual pleasure. A more androcentric, egocentric, and abusive form of sexism is hard to imagine.

~ ~ ~

And when the angels said, "Mary, God has chosen thee, and purified thee; He has chosen thee above all women. Mary, be obedient to thy Lord, prostrating and bowing before Him."
—Qur'an 3:37

This text suggests the veneration that Muslims might have for Mary, the Mother of Jesus. It also suggests that the docility expected of Muslim women has been rooted in the Lordship of a masculine deity.

Mary is a good Muslim — that is the first Islamic notion of her. As the virgin mother of Jesus, she served God's purposes and forwarded the history of salvation. Her conception of Jesus was miraculous, but nothing is impossible to Allah. Because he wished, Allah fertilized Mary's womb. Her great virtue was to accept God's purposes for her — to dispose herself in faith. She was a great believer, and her great belief led her to prostrate herself to God's will. The physical prostration enjoined on Mary in this text is an outward manifestation of the inward, spiritual prostration that she was to make in agreeing to the commission the angels brought to her.

The Qur'an (4:155) defends Mary and Jesus against calumnies it attributes to their Jewish opponents. The calumny against Mary was that her conception of Jesus was sinful and so his birth was illegitimate. The calumny against Jesus was that he died on the cross. In Muslim belief, only a likeness of Jesus died. Jesus himself did not die. This reminds us of the tangled relations to Judaism and Christianity that lie at the origins of Islam. Muhammad apparently knew many of the biblical stories. Islam came to think of Jews and Christians as "people of the book." As such, Jews and Christians were kin to Muslims and could enjoy special privileges in Muslim lands. But Jews refused to accept Islamic interpretations of the Bible, earning considerable enmity. And Christians persisted in declaring Jesus to be divine (though many Christians converted to Islam). So along with the admiration for Judaism and Christianity that one can intuit in the Qur'an runs the sense that they have been superseded. As well, when they oppose Islam vigorously they join the unbelievers.

Jews are unbelievers when they calumniate Mary as having brought Jesus forth through illicit sex. Christians are unbelievers when they insist that Jesus really died on the cross. But Christians and Muslims have much in common when they laud the obedience of Mary that led to the virgin birth of Christ. Let us pursue this common esteem for Mary into its patriarchal roots.

As obedient to God's will, no matter how apparently outlandish, Mary has served both Christians and Muslims as a model believer. As completely pure, untouched by any man, the Mary receiving the angelic announcement has also served both Christians and Muslims as a model of female chastity. We have seen the fixation that Islam has sometimes developed concerning women's chastity. One could find a similar fixation among certain Christian groups. So for both Christian and Muslim women Mary could be a two-edged sword. On the one hand, her faith could seem marvelous. On the other hand, because it was impossible to imitate her virginal motherhood, her role model could become oppressive.

Obedience and purity offered to God are one thing. Obedience and purity offered to a male deity by a young woman are another. And obedience and purity offered to human males by a young woman are a third. In the first instance, one can make the case that the creature is simply giving the Creator what is due. In the second case, one can think that picturing the deity as male colors the young woman's obedience and purity differently than it would be colored if offered to (or asked by) a female deity. In the third case, one can feel that the dangers of sexism run high, especially since there is probably no requirement that young men offer obedience and purity to a female deity. The nexus between the male deity and the human males is the key to the reflection I want to develop. Inasmuch as both God and men ask obedience

and purity of Muslim women, this raises the possibility that Muslims could think that men are God's images more than women
are.

Of course, we know that this possibility became an actually in
many eras of Muslim, Christian, and Jewish history. The feminist
notion that if God is a male then the male is God puts the result
in pithy form. So the virtue of Mary and other good Muslim
women could become part of a mosaic of patriarchal dominion.
By obeying Allah so wholeheartedly, Mary could ease the way
for women to think they ought to obey the men in their lives
wholeheartedly. Since Allah was a male, obeying human males
could seem natural and necessary.

Is Allah a male? Sophisticated Muslim theology would say no.
Allah is beyond the limitations that sexual differentiation intro-
duces. Anything that is positive in female existence must be found
in Allah, its source. But Muslim culture did not develop this intuition very much, as Jewish and Christian cultures did not. When
Muslims thought about Allah's governance of the world, they
tended to picture a Lord giving orders and determining results.
The metaphor involved depended on caliphs, sheiks, and other
male authority figures prominent in Muslim cultures. There was
no Lady serving as an alternate metaphor, because there were no
females wielding authority like that of caliphs and sheiks.

We shall see that Hinduism did better than Islam, Christianity,
and Judaism when it came to depicting the female component of
divinity. But we shall also see that this more feminine theology
did not liberate Hindu women socially or politically. So even
though the maleness of the Muslim deity could undergird male
supremacy, it probably did not create such supremacy. Probably
people construct their models for divinity more from their models
of human interactions than on the basis of a revelation bypassing
such interactions. That would imply that the primary determinant
of the male deity one finds in the Abrahamic faiths (Judaism,
Christianity, and Islam) has been the rule of men in the cultures
in which those faiths were located.

How could Muslim women escape the noxious possibilities in
a faith such as that which the Qur'an finds in Mary? Only by em-
igrating from their native cultures. It was not sufficient to argue

that Allah was no more male than female, or that Mary's obedience and purity were models for men as much as for women. Correct as those arguments might be, they ran afoul of the language of the Qur'an and the assumptions of patriarchal cultures. Women therefore had to deal with male authority from top to bottom. In their relations with both divinity and men, they were so expected to obey and be pure that these qualities became part and parcel of femininity. Along with their fertility, women were prized for their obedience and their purity. It was fine for them to be intelligent, as long as they did not challenge male authority. It was wonderful for them to be beautiful, or artistic, or wealthy. But the Qur'an made the crux of admirable femininity obedience and purity. They had done such great things for Mary, leading to the birth of Jesus, that all good Muslim women naturally would want to develop them.

There is another Mary, available in the New Testament. She takes up the cry of Hannah, her predecessor in Jewish faith, and sings about God's liberation of the poor (see Luke 1:46–55). This Mary is obedient to God, and she is pure, but she is also a fierce advocate of social justice. Her conception of Jesus delights her because it means that God has taken the side of people of low estate, like herself. The connection between Mary's Magnificat and the Beatitudes of Jesus (Luke 6:20–26) is quite direct.

This Lukan Mary had to strike members of the male establishment as dangerous. Christianity tried to tame her, and Islam ignored her revolutionary potential. But she is available to her present-day sisters and brothers as a strong reminder that obedience to God need not mean obedience to male authority figures. Indeed, she is available as the human analogue of a female deity whose passion for her children makes her a great champion of justice on every level, perhaps especially that of sexual equality.

~ ~ ~

O Prophet, when believing women come to thee, swearing fealty to thee upon the terms that they will not associate with God anything, and will not steal, nor commit adultery, nor slay their

children, nor bring a calumny they forge between their hands and their feet, nor disobey thee in aught honorable, ask God's forgiveness for them; God is All-forgiving, All-compassionate.
—Qur'an 60:14

This text deals with converts to Islam, whether Arab women who have not yet embraced the Prophet's teaching or women captured in battle. If they are believers — if they accept Allah and Muhammad — they can join the house of Islam. Here Islam is at its most catholic: belief alone is necessary for admission to the Muslim community. Race, nationality, age, sex, and all the other ways that we distinguish people are irrelevant. Were Islam to think through the implications of this catholicity, it could see that women are the equals of men in the one thing necessary for pleasing God and so revise its traditional patriarchalism.

Notice what women are to believe. In the first instance, they are to associate nothing with God. In other words, they are to foreswear idolatry. God is simply God. Nothing one can add to Allah amplifies or reduces his divinity. His divinity is the first principle, the fundamental reality. Everything else depends on it. So one cannot associate God with particular places, forms, or formulas. They are all derivative. God is his own exegesis. One has to be willing to let God be God. A Muslim is one trying to be willing. A Muslim is a person who submits wholeheartedly to the Godness, the mysteriousness, the primacy of Allah.

Associating anything with God is idolatry, the foremost sin. But idolatry can take many forms. People who worship stones, or who insist that Jesus was divine, or who make money the great treasure of their life are all idolaters. So are people who think they are orthodox, who would not violate the creed, but whose lives say otherwise. Adulterers, for example, place something before God. Their illicit pleasure means more to them than keeping God's command. So, practically, Allah is secondary in their lives. Were Allah primary, they would not commit adultery.

Women begging admission to the house of Islam have to be willing to make Allah primary. In all ways, he has to be their great treasure. Muhammad certainly castigated the adultery of men, but in both the Qur'an and other Muslim authorities sexual misconduct is associated with women more than men. Either adultery is more grievous when women commit it, or women are the sex more likely to be wanton. In either case, the issue of adultery is not put before men as sharply as it is put before women. Relatedly, women have no right to four husbands that would run parallel to men's right to four wives. Indeed, although Muslim men can marry non-Muslim women, Muslim women cannot marry non-Muslim men. The Qur'an is therefore not even-handed when it comes to adultery. It is wrong for both sexes, but the assumption is that women need more control to avoid adultery than men do. I doubt that the history of the sexes' behavior around the world justifies this assumption.

That women should not slay their children seems a natural requirement. Most likely the context is the pagan practice of exposing infants considered inconvenient, or for whom the parents feared they could not provide. The fact is that the majority of such infants have been female. In virtually all patriarchal cultures, Islamic included, infanticide falls more heavily on girls than boys, because boys are more prized. (Girls are considered a potential burden: one has to find a dowry for them and a husband.) The implications of this text for abortion are not fully clear. Traditionally Islam has allowed abortion up to 120 days, thinking that the time when God gives the soul that makes the conceptus human.

The calumny committed between women's hands and their feet is obscure. The necessity of obeying the Prophet in all honorable things is pellucid. Women wanting admission to Islam ought to be obedient to Muhammad comprehensively, since he was and is the mouthpiece of Allah. Inasmuch as Muhammad can be equated with the Qur'an (a far from complete equation), a complete fidelity to the Qur'an is also implied.

The concluding lines about the Prophet's asking forgiveness for the convert women are touching, as are the assurances that God is all-forgiving and all-compassionate. Some feminists might take umbrage at a man's presuming to beg forgiveness for women, but they will not have appreciated how Muhammad functions for all Muslims, men as much as women. Any special need that women might have for forgiveness is secondary to the need they share with men as simply fallible human beings. Sometimes the

God of Islam is depicted as a stern Judge, a Lord of the Worlds
whose will is so imperative that there seems little room for human
freedom. The many passages in the Qur'an that speak of the mercy
and compassion of Allah not only offset this impression but seem
more central. Allah gave the Qur'an as a mercy. In all of his dealings with human beings he is merciful, seeking to enlighten both
men and women and lead them all to the light.

The contemporary reflection that intrigues me is the freedom
that awaits feminists, men as much as women, when they take
such a view of divinity to heart. All people need God's forgiveness. That is a fundamental tenet of all the Abrahamic faiths. Only
God is holy. All human beings fail to measure up. To be sure, Islam speaks more of forgetfulness and weakness than of willful
sin. Nonetheless, it stands with its sibling faiths in underscoring
the need that human beings have of God's forgiveness.

Secular feminism has little to say about forgiveness, reconcilia-
tion, atonement. On the whole, it is a child of the Enlightenment,
still trying to live off the capital of autonomy and self-reliance.
Certainly, many feminist groups encourage women to express
their feelings, to love themselves, to come to terms with what in
their lives and selves displeases them. But few such groups focus
their efforts on a God who takes the initiative in offering forgiveness. The God of Islam, like the God of Judaism and Christianity,
is the first mover in the business of forgiveness. The grace of God
precedes the human desire for forgiveness, making it possible for
people to make a new start.

For what is the grace of God but God's own love, God's
own pledge of desire for us human beings and unconditional
acceptance of who and what we are? God's grace is God's self—
completely creative and good. To relate to this God is to open
oneself to a goodness one has never experienced from creatures.
The best of one's friends, lovers, or selves has been only a faint
reflection of the divine holiness. The divine holiness, we too seldom realize, is the divine reality. God is the one who is fully real,
completely perfected. And so God is the one, the only One, who
can take us as we actually are, needing nothing from us, wanting
only our flourishing. For God to forgive us is for us to come to
ourselves, finally see things clearly, and realize our neediness. In

that moment, when we can bear who and what we are, the grace of God holds us, like a tiny bird in God's hand, and blesses our being. From deep inside us, where God keeps loving us into existence, we feel an affirmation, a license to make a new start. The problem of believing in the God of the Qur'an, as in the God of the Bible, is not his majesty or strangeness but his goodness. Allah is all-forgiving. As soon as the Muslim, the believer-submitter, honors how things actually are, God blesses his or her being. I can see the forgiveness of God making fall away a thousand torments on the left and a thousand psychic wrinkles on the right, so that secular feminists might for the first time appreciate how a truly comprehensive liberation would feel.[8]

2

Hindu Texts

He found no joy; so, even today, one who is all alone finds no joy. He yearned for a second. He became as large as a man and a woman locked in close embrace. This self he split into two; hence arose husband and wife. Therefore, as Yajnavalkya used to observe: "Oneself is like half of a split pea." That is why this void is filled by woman. He was united with her and thence were born human beings.[1]

—Brhadaranyaka Upanishad 1.4.3

This text occurs in the early portion of an extended reflection on the origin of human consciousness. The Upanishads are the final portion of the Vedas, the primary Hindu scriptures. Traditionally, Hindus have thought of the Vedas as the work of enlightened sages who grasped the Truth of how reality is composed. From their visions, these sages passed on to other mortals the stories about the gods, the origin of the world, the arising of consciousness, the source of error, and the like that those mortals needed if they were to live well. Most scholars attribute this foundational layer of Indian culture to the heritage of the people ("Aryans") who began to infiltrate the subcontinent from the northwest early in the second millennium B.C.E. (Before the Common [Christian] Era). The culture of the native Indians received this Aryan infusion, and from the mixture of the two cultures developed classical Hinduism — the synthesis available by the middle of the first millennium B.C.E., when new views, such as those of the Mahavira (the founder of Jainism) and Gautama (the founder of Buddhism), arose. Our text perhaps dates to the eight

43

century B.C.E.[2] Let us first explicate its lines and then reflect on its present implications or suggestions.

The text anthropomorphizes the Self, the seat of conscious identity. We learn in prior verses that the Self came from the nothingness of death and hunger, as the fruit of a desire for a positive identity. But the Self was alone, facing nothing, having nothing over-against which to define himself or with which to share. Our verse describes how the Self overcame this original condition, diversified, and produced the sexuality that both divides humanity and makes human sharing possible.

First, the motive for the action that produced woman and sexuality was to gain joy. Joy does not flourish in solitude. Joy requires sharing. Second, the Self swelled to the size and form of a present-day human couple embracing (sexually). Then it split into two. The closeness of the two parts that had been united was that of marital partners — people oriented to one another for a common being, life, and fertility. "Husband" and "wife" carry these overtones. Deep in the Hindu psyche lodged the notion that men and women need each other in all ways. This notion sometimes conflicted with yogic and ascetic impulses to flee from sexual union, but it remained a powerful support for marriage. Inasmuch as human nature was bisexual, the communion of men and women could be taken for granted and assumed to be good.

Yajnavalkya is a sage prominent in Upanishadic tradition. His observation here offers another figure for the original union of what is now the two halves of humanity, the female and male. In picturing the original humanity that was split, Yajnavalkya sees it as round like a pea. The two halves both have a 180 degree curve of humanity, a wide range of human qualities, but each lacks a complementary 180 degree curve. Whether the two curves are mirror images, obverse and reverse, is open to discussion. From the figure alone one cannot say. While Yajnavalkya probably meant to stress the mutual need of men and women, his image can also be taken to imply that women have as full a side of humanity, as full an arc of human qualities, as men.

Speaking from the male side, and continuing the male viewpoint that it assumed from the outset, when it first gave the Self a voice, the text says that woman fills the void of solitude that man suffers. By uniting with woman, man overcomes his isolation — doubly so. He returns to the aboriginal unity of the at least potentially androgynous whole that the Self made when it wanted to contend with primeval nothingness. And he also produces offspring, who further reduce his solitude.

The logic here is poetic and pictorial, more than rigorous. The main point is clear, however. Humanity as we now know it coordinates the two sexes. In their inclination toward one another breathes a nostalgia for an original unity, when they were not differentiated. By coming together, they defend themselves against solitude and joylessness. In coming together, they enjoy, at least momentarily, the oneness they had at the beginning. Moreover, their coming together is fruitful, creative. The human things arising from their union certainly are children, but also the ideas and artifacts, the cultural complexes, deriving from the overall, pervasive interaction of masculinity and femininity. Joy and fertility, as we now know them, depend on the coordination of men and women.

When one steps back from this ancient poetry to consider the thoughts it might stimulate nowadays, certainly the reflections about heterosexuality that feminism has generated may come to mind. Inasmuch as lesbian thought has been a powerful force in feminist theory and practice, heterosexuality sometimes comes in for close scrutiny, if not antagonistic challenge. Separatist lesbians want to limit contact with men and live quite independently. Less radical lesbians may admit the centrality of heterosexuality, and have no special animus against men, simply judging that what holds sway in the mainstream does not fit them personally. Naturally, one could develop a counterpart to female homosexual theory from male homosexuality. Sufficient for the moment, though, is the interaction between our text and female homosexual sensibilities.

Any feminist would notice the male bias of the text, and most feminists would probably attribute it to the patriarchy of the Aryans credited with the Vedas. They were a mobile, warlike people whose main deities were male. Like the ancient Europeans, with whom they seem to have shared many linguistic and cultural characteristics, they were oriented more toward the sky than to-

ward the earth. Nonetheless, they venerated the earth, as we shall
see, calling her the Great Mother. At any rate, whatever the in-
tricacies of cultural provenance, the dominance of the male voice
throughout the Vedas is clear. In our text, it determines that the
woman should be considered the supplement of the man. He is
the one suffering want and she is the one who fills it. So, she appears to serve his needs, while he appears as humanity in its first
instance — the one whose needs determine things. We have to
imagine any needs that she may have and any obligations he may
have to fulfill them. The text does not say whether it is legitimate
to reunite the two halves of the pea from either side — whether
it makes as much sense to rejoin man to woman as woman to
man. The otherness of the heterosexuality we see here focuses
principally on the woman. When humanity became bisexual, the
feminine side was the new or initially alien thing. The male side
was closer to humanity-in-itself or humanity's core component.
Insofar as feminism means the proposition that women are as
fully human as men, feminists must reject this Vedic depiction
of the human condition.

But must they reject heterosexuality? Granted its male bias,
the text still hints at a significant truth. Just as Plato (Sympo-
sium, 189e) and Genesis (2:21–23) created figures designed to
show the original unity of the sexes, so this Upanishadic text is
groping to understand the mutual attraction and need that a great
many men and women have felt through the ages as something
deeply embedded in human nature. Because so many people of
both sexes have found the other sex fascinating, and because the
two sexes must unite to procreate, heterosexuality tends to be
taken as the norm and homosexuality as the less usual inclination or option. At the moment, I am not interested in the moral
implications of this judgment. At the moment, what strikes me
more strongly is the suggestion of this canonical Hindu text that
heterosexuality is encoded in human nature for the joy and com-
pletion of both sexes. To the extent that this is true, it implies
that feminism should not be antagonistic to masculinity. What
that extent is can be debated, and one should add that feminism
by definition has to oppose biases giving masculinity more rights
than femininity. But the mysteriousness of heterosexual attrac-

tion seems to me both a fact and a grace — a fact and a grace
that I want no defense of lesbianism, however valid, to mock or
diminish. To the extent that it celebrates the positive aspects of
heterosexuality, this text is a boon to all readers.

~   ~   ~

*Yajnavalkya said, "Gargi, do not question too much, lest your
head fall off. In truth, you are questioning too much about a
divinity about which further questions cannot be asked. Gargi,
do not over-question."* [3]

—Brhadaranyaka Upanishad 3.6

Yajnavalkya is the same sage that we met in our first Upanishadic
text. Gargi Vacaknavi is one of the most famous women in the
Upanishadic literature, immortalized for her relentless questioning of the sage. It is she who presses him to the limit, searching for
the ultimate foundation of the world. Two features of her Upanishadic profile deserve comment. First, the simple fact that she is
a prominent figure in a key dialogue suggests that in early Indian
culture women could be important intellectuals. In later Indian
culture, women were so circumscribed and so badly educated,
that a performance such as Gargi's would have been unthinkable.
Second, by making Gargi the object lesson in its instruction that
there is a limit to fruitful questioning, the Upanishadic literature
established or reenforced the stereotype that women are too curious. To some extent, the text pays Gargi a great compliment.
Questioning so as to gain wisdom about the ultimate foundations of reality is the hallmark of the most honored sage, the
one whose liberation comes from intellectual insight. Whereas
the classical yogin abandoned the mind, trying to gain the evac-
uated consciousness known as *samadhi*, where one would simply
be or live the truth that ultimate reality and particular reality are
identical, the sage *saw* this truth — perceived it mentally, in a
flash of insight that transformed his (or her) whole personality.
The advantage the sage had over the yogin was that the sage could

teach others and work out the implications of such insight (the structures of the world).

The wisdom that Yajnavalkya finally would impart to Gargi is intriguing. At the end of its questioning, the mind must stop, pivot, and let silence be its guide. Questioning, searching for answers, is valuable but limited. Because it is an exercise of the discursive mind, the ratiocinative dimension of human spirituality, it can neglect more holistic matters. When the mind stops, because it intuits that the "answer" it is seeking is too simple, too primordial, to yield itself up to discursive reason, the silence that confronts it becomes a new, more comprehensive language. That is what Gargi has to learn. Arguably, she is no different from a diligent male inquirer in having to learn it. Arguably, it is not her sex but her immaturity (suggested by her status as a student, rather than a guru in her own right) that explains why she has not yet learned it. Still, by putting this praiseworthy but immature intellectual searching in the person of a female disciple, the text may slide over into stereotype.

The world over, the stereotype is that women are curious and talky. Somewhat relatedly, the stereotype is that women should listen to men if they want to learn about what truly matters. For lovers of wisdom, inquiry is a mixed blessing. On the one hand, without a hunger to learn, there will be no significant progress. On the other hand, until one realizes that questioning orients one to the mystery of being and creation, one's questioning will bring diminishing returns. Gargi is the ideal student when it comes to diligence, but does her female nature make her slow to recognize the limits of questioning — the need to contemplate simply and comprehensively, from the heart?

Stereotypes notwithstanding, the fact seems to be that women are at least as inclined to recognize the holistic, more than verbal or intellectual, character of ultimate reality as men. Indeed, the counter-stereotype is that women recognize the primacy of love, the most comprehensive human response to the mystery of existence, more quickly and naturally than men. To be sure, stereotypes do as much harm as good. Letting them cancel one another here, I want to stress the courage that Gargi showed in forcing Yajnavalkya to give her the ultimate insight: knowing that one cannot know, cannot control, the ultimate mystery of existence.

In their exchanges prior to the climax that our text records, Yajnavalkya has tried to pacify Gargi with penultimate answers. The world is composed of water, and behind water wind, and behind wind atmosphere — so does Yajnavalkya regress along the chain of causes. Only at the end, when he is exasperated enough to spit out the full truth, does it emerge that he cannot really say what the world is made of. And if he cannot say, no one can, for he is the sage of sages.

Why did he not tell Gargi this from the beginning? Perhaps because only the knowledge that is hard-won, that comes from a relentless march down the chain of causes, will be appreciated as truly significant. The Hindu gurus realized that they would do their students no favors by revealing the deepest truths prematurely. Gargi was the ideal student because she kept pushing for a truly satisfying answer. If she was surprised that the truly satisfying answer turned out to be negative, our text does not record it. It may be, then, that what the sage finally admitted had been her intuition for a long time, if not from the beginning. It may be that she had known in her bones that nothing so partial as human speech could capture the true nature of things.

The true nature of things is mysterious. Any brothers Gargi may have had could gain this ultimate revelation along stereotypical male routes. They could find that none of their ambition or aggression or diligent study trying to storm the castles of truth did the job. But Gargi and her sisters would have had their own paths to this insight. In addition to her work with the sage, her guru, Gargi would have had the experience that there was no full justice in Indian society. The poor, and women, and others generally existing on the margins of Indian cultural power all knew, in their blood, that their social order was imperfect. To justify their lives, they had to open themselves to a more than customary plan, an order that was simpler or richer than human beings could imagine. Similarly, Gargi and her sisters would have experienced bodily, in the periodicity of their somatic rhythms, that existence did not follow straight lines, and that the body, representing material reality, did not submit completely to the mind, representing spiritual reality. Everything was more complicated, or paradoxical, than the ratiocinative, discursive mind wanted and expected. Everything was more mysterious.

Seeing Gargi as embracing Yajnavalkya's final answer joyously, as a ratification of her best intuition, I like to make her a model of feminine wisdom. Feminine wisdom is content to let the final order and sense of reality repose with God, who keeps it like an infant growing in her womb. When time has matured to God's full pleasure, it will give birth to a cosmic destiny justifying the way that God has gestated it. Prior to that consummating time, the part of human wisdom is to attend honestly, in full confession that one does not understand but is bedazzled.

The world is bedazzling. Always and everywhere, there is too much to understand, too much beauty to appreciate fully, too much pain and need to bear. Wisdom entails accepting this simple fact and learning to be invigorated by it. The mystery that saves humankind is a darkness, an infinity, a plenitude of mind and being that overwhelms us and yet all the while is our best companion, our strongest nourishment, our dearest succor. I like to think that Gargi clapped her hands and kissed the sage, because she had finally gotten him to admit what she had suspected for years.

~ ~ ~

To Earth belong the four directions of space. On her grows food; on her the ploughman toils. She carries likewise all that breathes and stirs. Earth, may she grant us cattle and food in plenty.[4]
—Atharva Veda 12.1.4

Scholarly consensus has no doubt that the Vedas are considerably older than the Upanishads. Indeed, some scholars place the oldest portions of the Vedas, the Rig-Veda and Artharva-Veda, as far back as 2000–1700 B.C.E.[5] At that time agriculture was still full of wonders. People had learned to till the soil, but they continued to think of the growth of crops in the earth as their gestation in a motherly deity. Often the pervasive mythology made mother earth the partner of father sky. The main function of father sky in the creation of food was to send down fertilizing rain, which was likened to semen. The rest of the process, more hidden and significant, occurred in darkness, as the seed slowly ripened within the bosom of the earth, the universal mother.

The four directions of space create a mandala — a powerfully symbolic form. Whether in the pattern of a cross, or a swastika (an ancient Indo-European symbol), or a circle bisected into quadrants, the four directions could stand for the totality of existence. One finds this among ancient peoples in many lands. Native Americans, for example, would pray to the four directions when they sought purification in the sweat lodge. Sometimes people added two other directions, above and below, making the mandala three-dimensional. Even without this addition, however, the comprehensive character of the directions was plain.

Later Indian thought tended to equate material reality with the feminine principle and spiritual reality with the masculine principle. Perhaps the beginnings of this outlook lay in the ancient distinction between father sky and mother earth. The gestation of mother earth was more physical, dirtier, than the insemination by father sky. It was more rooted and embodied. Interestingly, later Indian thought also made the feminine principle more active than the masculine principle. The ideal of the impassive, self-sufficient yogi (who was almost always male) suggested that passion, dependence, and change were a feminine counterpoint to a male detachment and serenity. Thus, it developed that the feminine principle had a more obvious role in creativity, whence change burst forth dramatically, energetically, like the arrival of a child from the womb. The masculine principle was involved in a creativity that was more cerebral and passive: when Brahman (ultimate reality) vouchsafed the vision allowing the sage to perceive things as they most truly were, the sage was perhaps 90 percent a passive (though prepared) participant, perhaps only 10 percent active.

The toiling of the ploughman struck ancient Indians, and many other peoples caught in the wonders of agriculture, as like the male role in human conception. It may not be certain how fully ancient Indians understood the biology of human procreation, but they certainly realized that sexual intercourse played a key part. In some yogic schools this realization led to the sacralization of sex. Visualizing themselves as father sky and mother earth, an earthly couple could have sexual relations as an act of worship directed toward the life-force. The giant sculptures of human genitalia that one finds going back millennia into the Indian past represent a dramatic sacralization of the life-force. The male organ (*lingam*) and the female organ (*yoni*) both stand for something mysterious, holy, divine.

Inasmuch as patriarchal judgments predominated over egalitarian ones, women could be subordinate to the strivings of males who wanted to make the life-force serve their own enlightenment and liberation from *samsara* (the endless cycle of deaths and rebirths). On the other hand, some of the schools that went in for dramatic rituals such as sacralized sex (the generic name for those schools is *tantrist*) saw that women's sexuality was as necessary and holy as men's and so granted women considerable equality. Still, even tantrist women could be considered more means to a male end than people equally apt for liberation from *samsara*. Indeed, in mainstream Hindu reflection about *samsara* it became axiomatic that women could escape *samsara* only in a lifetime when they had been reborn as men.

The rest of our text suggests that the Aryans venerated mother earth as a goddess, and through verse after verse this Veda multiplies praises for the gifts of so bountiful a mother. In thinking about the significance of such a text for American culture at the end of the twentieth century C.E., almost four thousand years from the time when people of India were reciting hymns such as this, I am struck by the text's reverence for the earth and human sexuality. The earth is very much a living parent. Human sexuality, far from being something to snigger at, is a primordial wonder. Indeed, the large stratum of Hindu theology (reflection on divinity) that retains sexuality in the most ultimate reality (for example, by giving all the leading gods, male and female alike, marital partners) suggests that the creativity one finds running throughout earthly creation is a fine analogue for what goes on in heavenly creation.

The ecological implications of the reverence for mother earth are obvious. Until we restore wonder and gratitude for the source of our food and sustenance, for the matrix on which all human life depends, we will not overturn our present ways, which manifestly are geocidal. We are killing the earth — the soil, the air, the waters, the animals, the forests. Our present industrial way of life runs by a biology, a chemistry, a nuclear physics, and a technology in such leading industries as the automobile that are incompatible with the ecosystems of our planet. Be these local, small-scale ecosystems or global, comprehensive ecological patterns (for example, of the winds and seas), they are all in peril. I think that nothing will change until we are dragged, polluted and choking, to repent of our disparagement of mother earth and be converted to lifestyles that give mother earth a radical primacy. Until the ecological survival of the plant becomes the top priority of our ways of life, our children and grandchildren will live under an awful cloud.

It is interesting to speculate that the converted lifestyles we require would be healthier regarding sex than were the nineteenth- and twentieth-century lifestyles from which our currently disastrous patterns emerged. The Victorian era is famous for its repression of sexuality, off which Freud made his reputation, while the current spread of a "therapeutic" culture throughout middle-class America (the counseling industry) regularly suggests how much is wrong with relations between the sexes nowadays. No doubt, the causes of our widespread malaise, a central part of which is sexual, are many and their interconnection is complex. But under the stimulus of this Vedic text I find the hypothesis that when the earth is not a bounteous, fertile mother, both men and women lose their sexual footing.

For, approached in a contemplative spirit, sexuality continues to be a great mystery. The great advances that we have made in understanding the genetics and biology of procreation have not answered the more basic question: why should survival have taken this route? As well, they have not answered the question of sexual attraction among human animals, which is so much more than the rut of Spring. Anyone who looks closely, with a fresh mind, at a newborn has to catch a breath or skip a heartbeat. When a tiny baby wiggles its perfect fingers or seems to smile, the wise are awestruck. Were this awe to flow over into our evaluations of human sexuality and the bounty of the earth, as it seems to have done for the typical ancient Indian, we would know why we have to make love rather than war, or more ugly power plants, or more dubious chemicals. We would know why we have to shift from our insensitive, materialistic view of the earth to a view that would replace destructive technology with the music, prayer, poetry, basic science, and sexual freedom that do not violate the earth and can laud it properly.

~ ~ ~

The onslaught of the Goddess caused terrible bloodshed among the demons and resulted in a scene of gruesome carnage. Mortally wounded victims vomited blood, while some looked like porcupines having been wounded with so many arrows. Severed arms, legs, and heads littered the battlefield. Her victims jerked in the throes of death and appeared to be performing a macabre dance of death. The battlefield was so strewn with wreckage of the demon army, and so flooded with blood, that it was nearly impassable. As a raging fire consumes fields and forests, so the Goddess devastated the ranks of the demon army.[6]
—Devi-mahatmya 2.60–67

The larger text from which these verses come celebrates the glories of the Great Goddess. For although Hinduism has honored many different goddesses, it has also combined them into a single female representation of divinity. The Great Goddess is like the sum total of all the attributes that the individual goddesses manifest. Indian theology has been less concerned with logical consistencies than Western theology. It has been happy to live with the ambiguity of letting Durga or Sita or Lakshmi seem to stand for all feminine divinity while yet specializing in destroying evil, or personifying wifely virtue, or meting out good fortune. The partial has implied the total, and the total has been hinted in the partial. Thus Durga, the goddess hymned in these verses, is the Great Goddess in her work of destroying evil.

For many ancient peoples, mother earth not only brought forth new life, she received back spent life. She was not only the universal womb but also the universal tomb. Eventually, all things returned to the humus from which they had come. So mother earth was a bipolar deity. Nothing so simple as sheer goodness or sheer evil explained her character adequately. She was both the beginning and the end. One had to fear her as well as reverence her, for she presided over death as well as life.

It is important to note that Durga is bloodthirsty, awesomely destructive, because she is raging against the demons. The proper response to evil influences is an anger determined to wipe them out. One can say, then, that the Great Mother is here defending the interests of her devotees, her children. The demons want to torture human beings, either by keeping them chained to *samsara* or by afflicting them in hells after their deaths. Durga is comfortable with blood and skulls. She wears them as signs of her ability to overcome the most fearful foes haunting the human imagination.

When Hindu texts describe the vengeances of male gods, they can pile up striking images one after another. But seldom do they deal so graphically as the texts that describe the vengeances of female gods. Perhaps this relates to the perception we noted earlier that the female principle was considered more active, wilder. Perhaps it also relates to the female association with blood. The blood of birth is inseparable from the blood of menstruation and death. All three occasions of bloodshed rendered an ancient Indian polluted — in need of sacrifice before being able to come before the sacred powers without fear. We may consider Durga to be in part a great projection of a deep-seated uneasiness with blood. By creating what is almost a cartoon, Indians were able to externalize their fears and so handle them better.

What have we present-day Americans done with our fears of death and blood? How have we managed to exorcize them? Answers could vary, but many commentators think we have a lot more work to do before we will be able to make death as natural as it ought to be. Perhaps death can never seem completely natural. Perhaps a mighty "no!" will and should always break out of the human throat. Nonetheless, for the foreseeable future we shall continue to die. Therefore, we shall continue to need myths and rituals that help us to deal with our fears of death. Strangely enough, scenes such as this one of Durga rampaging in battle seem to have proven helpful in Indian history. (The parallel in Christian history might be the comfort that millions have drawn from contemplating the crucified Christ.) By naming this great enemy, myths and rituals get people's fears out of the interior darkness, where they tend to fester.

What is the peculiar potency in having a female deity represent the power of death? Positively, it may be that any representative of the Great Goddess is also a representative of the Great Mother and so automatically a figure of hope and comfort. Negatively, or ambiguously, it may be that male sages have projected onto female divinities their deep-seated uneasiness with the otherness of women. Men can never understand women fully, as women can never understand men. Even when we agree that men cannot understand men fully, or that women cannot understand women fully, sexual difference remains a significant divide. Psychologically, this difference is nearly bound to be expressed when it comes to dealing with evil, suffering, and death, the most troubling aspects of the human condition. Psychologically, the natural ties between birth and death make it nearly inevitable that the feminine principle will seem more extreme, less normal, than the male. To be sure, a patriarchal cultural context, in which men run most institutions and so think of themselves as the first instance of human nature, contributes to this perception of women as more extreme (both more holy and more depraved, both sweeter and wilder). But the somewhat independent workings of the psyche seem to play a role also. When they thought about the most significant, ultimate implications of femininity (what the female would be, were she raised to the power of divinity), traditional Hindus gave females stronger associations with death, as well as life, than they gave males.

The Abrahamic faiths, as I have called them, fought against fertility goddesses and loathed the notion of placing femininity or sexual activity in God. No doubt the Bible's polemic against the fertility deities of Canaan was in part a matter of cultural dissonance (trying to make the ways of the people they had to conquer seem repugnant). It must also have been in part a matter of patriarchal males wanting to be sure that divinity reflected them more than women, because such a greater reflection would help them maintain control. But one of the perverse side-effects of this polemic against femininity in the godhead was great difficulty in taming death.

To attack this difficulty, the Abrahamic faiths forgot their fears of divine femininity and let in through the back door such stereotypically female virtues as compassion, mercy, caring more for the pain of sinners than their legal transgressions. Of course, the profile of men can include compassion, mercy, and unconditional love, but in most cultures, including the ancient Indian, the profile of women was richer in these virtues. So in most cultures, the divinity as stereotypically feminine could take the dying to her bosom, just as she had brought them forth at their birth. In Roman Catholic Christianity, this desire seems to have played a large part in the commission of the dying to the care of Mary, the mother of Jesus. As the primary Marian prayer, the "Hail Mary," puts it: "Holy Mary, mother of God, pray for us sinners now and at the hour of our death."

The qualities that medical personnel trying to help the plight of terminally ill patients tend to stress include love of self and positive imagery about the meaning that even death can carry.[7] To discover such a positive meaning, one has to turn over the gruesome imagery of Durga in our verses and show its psychic counterbalance. Yet that is not difficult to do. To fight against demons is to fight for the good. To control the fate of demons, presiding over life and death, is to present oneself as a great source of help. The traditional Hindus who prayed to Durga probably experienced considerable fear, but they may also have experienced considerable joy. For hundreds of years, they have contemplated scenes such as those from our text, and one can argue that they would not have done so had such scenes not given them reasons to hope. Durga, then, suggests how the sacrality of the feminine, complex though it be, has remained a mainstay of Hindu psychological stability.

~ ~ ~

*With the disruption of the family, the eternal family tradition
perishes. With the collapse of the tradition chaos overtakes the
whole race. Such predominance of chaos leads to the corruption
of women in the family. When the women are corrupted the
whole society erodes.*[8]

—Bhagavad-Gita 1:40–41

The Bhagavad-Gita is probably the most famous Hindu scripture.
Integrated into the gigantic epic poem the Mahabharata around
the third century B.C.E., it presents teachings of the god Krishna
to the troubled warrior Arjuna. These verses are part of Arjuna's
opening lament, when he realizes that he is expected to fight
against his relatives (the Mahabharata deals with a great prehis-
toric war between two of the leading Indian families, who were
related). Eventually Krishna will instruct Arjuna how to recon-
cile himself to the duties of his warrior caste. For the moment,
however, the spotlight is on the social destruction that war can
bring.

Note how conservative these verses are. Arjuna thinks that
family traditions are the basic defense against social chaos. To
understand his view, we have to think in terms of the extended
family, and realize that for ancient societies such as the Indian
the family included the departed ancestors. One's kin, present
and past, were one's basic defenses against the troubles that life
could bring. For the family to be upset, to lose its longstanding
patterns, was terribly threatening. Tradition, then, was not a dead
letter. Tradition was the wisdom passed down from prior generations, whom it had served well. Naturally, people were bound
to change some practices that they had inherited, because new
situations were bound to arise and make them adjust. But traditional peoples have been remarkable for the degree to which
they have preferred to reinterpret tradition rather than jettison it.
Arjuna is a representative traditional Indian in thinking that the
disruption of family life and tradition that war is bound to bring
is disastrous.

The chaos unleashed by war strikes even at women, who are
not combatants. And when it does strike women, the family structure that is the basic building block of society crumbles. Many

of the limits that ancient societies placed on women's activity stemmed from this conviction. If women stepped outside their accustomed roles, then children and family life would run amok. We have seen that the Muslim profile of the ideal wife makes her obedient and chaste. No doubt Arjuna has a similar profile in mind when he thinks about what war might do to Hindu women. If it were to remove their traditional subordination to men, even if only because their fathers, husbands, and sons were away from home or had died in war, it would upset the natural order and bring grave consequences. If warfare were to expose women to threats to their chastity, more disorders would ensue. The lines of descent so important to traditional families would be polluted. Children and society at large might not know who the true fathers were. So, "when the women are corrupted, the whole society erodes." That puts the ancient Indian view in a nutshell.

It is curious, of course, that so many societies have thought this way about women and yet failed to give women rights equal to those of men. It is curious that the mainstay of the family, and so of the society at large, should be subject to direction from male relatives from cradle to grave. Conveniently, the male authorities could say at one and the same time that women were the key to domestic order and that women were also flighty or loose and so needed constant control.

The judgment about the crucial role of women in most households was simply a matter of common sense. Inasmuch as they brought forth the children, raised them, served the meals, obtained the clothing, did much of the nursing, paid homage to the household deities thought responsible for good fortune, and interceded to smooth many emotional frictions, women obviously were the ones who sustained the household. The men had to work the fields or run the shops. The domestic responsibilities of the men were limited to the quarter of the life cycle when they were expected to work in the world and so experience for themselves the truths of tradition about the need for detachment, meditation, and the like. In the ideal male life cycle, one studied with a guru before marriage and then, when one saw one's grandchildren, was free to withdraw from domestic and public life to prepare one's spirit for death. Wives might join their husbands in this withdrawal, but husbands had no obligation to take their wives along. Moreover, when their husbands died Indian women were at the mercy of their extended families (at marriage they had moved to their husband's family). The poor, neglected widow is one of the stock figures of Indian tragedy. Thus, many Indian women performed countless rituals to ensure their husbands' long lives. All of this female activity obviously made women the center of domestic life.

The judgment that women always needed male control is much less obvious, but it is deeply rooted in Indian history. As noted, women were considered more physical and less spiritual than men. They were thought to be ruled by emotion rather than reason. With the exception of a few famous women such as Gargi, the "upper" ranges of Indian culture were exclusively a male preserve. Men were the priests, the gurus, the rulers, the farmers and traders. Women worked very hard, both at home and in agriculture or business, but their first responsibility was to produce offspring to continue the family line.

On their own, women in many cultures have formed the opinion that what corrupts society is not the looseness of females but the wars and other aggressions of men. The text we have here could support this view, but only if one made Arjuna wiser than Krishna. For Krishna tells Arjuna that caste responsibility is so important that he has to fight regardless of the consequences. And he also tells Arjuna that there is no real killing or being killed, because the human spirit is the real self and the body is quite secondary. One can imagine that this teaching went down badly with many women, whose major reason to be was to bring forth new embodied spirits.

Lack of education may have been the primary reason that most Indian women did not follow refined spiritual paths such as those laid out in the first part of the Bhagavad-Gita, but a resistance to denigrating the physical may also have played a part. Women tended to worship and advance spiritually through what Hinduism has called *bhakti*: devotional love. The final chapters of the Gita praise this spiritual path, culminating in the revelation that the devotees of Krishna (the majority of whom have been women) are dear to him. It is interesting that in following the path of *bhakti* Indian women were both verifying the stereotype that their gift was for emotion rather than reason and challenging the depreciation that most male estimates of their gift carried. Indian women, like their sisters in most other cultures, have not wanted to be detached and cerebral as their male counterparts often strove to be. They have sensed, in their hearts, wombs, and minds, that truth has to be warm as well as lucid, round as well as linear, something to feel as well as something to judge. This holism has been women's salvation, helping them to live longer than men and avoid most of the aggression that has thrown societies out of kilter everywhere. So the judgment of this text is correct, but much more ambiguous than what appears on the surface. If women are corrupted into thinking like men about warfare and truth, social chaos will indeed result. If women can continue to embody attractive alternatives to warfare and rationalism, they may stave off chaos for another generation.

~   ~   ~

Where women are honoured, there the gods are pleased; but where they are not honoured, no sacred rite yields rewards.... Though destitute of virtue, or seeking pleasure (elsewhere), or devoid of good qualities, (yet) a husband must be constantly worshipped as a god by a faithful wife.[9]
—Manu 3:56, 5:154

Manu is the name given to the author of the code of laws most influential in Hindu history. The name itself means "man" and functions somewhat like "Adam." Manu therefore claims to be the legislation that human nature itself postulates. Although this code never gained the status of the Vedic literature, it could be more influential than the Vedas, because more practical. Hindu law has been a compound of religious ideal and pragmatic necessity. In its views of how Indian women ought to live, Manu is thoroughly ambiguous. As our two verses suggest, on the one hand women should be honored, because they are part of the scheme of things that the gods have created. On the other hand, women ought always to be subject to men, and their devotion to their husbands ought to verge on worship. When one adds that several texts in Manu consider women deeply sinful, one has a dangerous situation. Unless Manu were interpreted with a large spirit (indeed, with a true love of women), it could become strongly misogynistic.

That is the difficulty that feminists find with many canonical texts. They depend on a generous spirit, an antecedent fondness for women, to work against the letter of their negative pronouncements about women. Thus, they are hopeless unless something more interior is recognized as more authoritative. To put it bluntly, a Hindu reader would have to say "nonsense!" to the misogynism latent in the rule that women ought always to be controlled. Otherwise, the rule could become women's incarceration. In fact, sometimes it was women's incarceration, severely limiting what women could do, where they could go, and what they could think. Women had to depend on the generosity of the men to whom they were supposedly subject if the women were to have any sense of liberty. That is a dangerous state of affairs, and one contradicted by the feminist intuition that women are as fully human as men (and so as responsible for their own destinies and the destiny of the race).

The verses we use here do not contradict one another, though they do run in different directions. The first verse makes a link between honoring women and being blessed by the gods. The logic is that the gods want women to be honored. Why? The text does not say. From Hindu tradition in general one can conjecture that (a) the gods have ordered social life (so that women be honored), (b) women's fertility makes them important to the gods, and (c) men and women are so ordered to one another that unless both are honored their common enterprise will founder.

The second verse makes it clear that women's obligations to men are more strenuous than men's obligations to women. Women are to venerate their husbands regardless of how their husbands behave. At times this blank check could include physical abuse. The assumption seems to be that the wife is ordained to serve the husband and take her lead from him in all things. She could be obedient and chaste as the tradition wanted her to be only if she venerated her husband like a god. No lesser degree of devotion could assure her success in the roles of wife and mother.

One might tolerate this second verse, calling it mere hyperbole, were there a parallel verse bidding husbands to venerate their wives as goddesses. We have mentioned the tantric rituals in which men and women united sexually in imitation of the gods and goddesses. Perhaps such rituals carried a seed of equality in the two sexes' veneration of one another. But the law codes such as Manu did not bring this seed to flower. In them Indian patriarchy held sway, sometimes to virulent effect. For they inculcated a fear of women, as impediments to men's spiritual growth, and the instinct that men had to control all of society, because women were tainted and untrustworthy.

The laws of a culture are only one indication of how people think and act, of course, so we should not assume that classical Hindu society had no marriages in which a de facto equality, based on a mutual affection, flourished. Moreover, women had outlets in religion (many rituals, pilgrimages, and associations peculiar to themselves) that could keep up their spirits. On the other hand, because their marriages were arranged and their destiny was limited to the vocation of wife and mother, traditional Hindu women had to work hard to win their husbands over to their cause. Often they were battling their mother-in-law for their husband's affection and allegiance, and they were under great pressure to produce male children. Indeed, some of that pressure came from their own needs: until they had children, especially sons, whose loyalty they could bind to themselves, they controlled few assets in the game of domestic politics.

From classical Hindu literature, such as the Ramayana, Hindu women learned that the lot of even the perfect wife, Sita (consort of Rama, one of the several incarnations of Vishnu [Krishna is the other most important one]), was painful. Although Sita was faithful to Rama through thick and thin, he doubted her and caused her much suffering. Eventually Sita despaired of winning Rama's trust and let herself die, achieving in death an equality denied her in life (her dying wounded Rama as deeply as his distrust had wounded her). While Indian women might internalize the perfect devotion of Sita, who did indeed serve her husband as a god, they had to be leery of what such perfect devotion would get them. Very easily they could become the pawns of their husbands, subject to the husbands' whims. Still, it was so much better to be married than single or widowed that most Hindu women have been willing to put up with a great deal. Indeed, one of the best explanations for the practice of *sati* (widow-burning, outlawed for centuries, but still occurring occasionally) is that the widow felt she had nothing left to live for. On the other end of the spectrum, the high incidence of deaths among newly married women in recent times has been attributed to several dismal phenomena. Being educated, the women could well have become depressed by the circumscription of their prospects that came with marriage and subjection to both husband and mother-in-law. Even worse, some commentators think that husbands have killed their young wives, because, having received a handsome dowry at the time of marriage, they had reaped most of the benefit they sought.

So in many pockets of Hindu society the honor of women has not balanced the honor that women were expected to give to men. In most periods of history, women have not gotten a fair shake. It is not even clear that women could expect a complete restitution of justice after death. While the Hindu goddesses were powerful, the more sophisticated Hindu views of afterlife did not have human beings taken to the bosom of the Great Mother but spoke rather of the extinction of personal identity. Beatitude after death would come from escaping from one's karmic bonds and entering a state called *moksha*. Women could hope to gain *moksha* (after having been reborn as men), and *moksha* would be worth any sufferings they might have endured. But whether *moksha* would declare the basic equality of women with men, or somehow punish men for their sexist abuses of women, is uncertain. Little in Hindu literature suggests that it would. Present-day American women therefore may look upon traditional Hindu women as good examples of what happens when there is no feminist movement. Women are at the mercy of male benevolence, and that can prove disastrous.

3

Buddhist Texts

I, Lord, for life want to give to the Order cloths for the rains, food for those coming in (to monasteries), food for those going out, food for the sick, food for those who nurse them, medicine for the sick, a constant supply of conjey, and bathing cloths for the Order of nuns.[1]

—Vinaya-pitaka I, 291

This text comes from the canon of Buddhist scriptures written in Pali and especially treasured by the Theravadin Buddhists. The Theravadins claim to represent the oldest traditions. Here the speaker is a woman named Visakha, who came to serve as a model of lay devotion. She was wealthy, and by putting her resources at the service of the Buddha's monastic community ("order"), she functioned as the ideal layperson, supporting the spiritual work of the monks and nuns from her material plenty. The Lord to whom Visakha addresses her request to provide material helps to the order is Gautama, the Buddha himself. Having gained enlightenment when he was about forty, he spent the last half of his life as a wandering teacher, establishing his order and showing monks, nuns, and laypeople the Middle Path — the way to deliverance from *samsara*.

Visakha is presented as a devout Indian woman of the early fifth century B.C.E. (Gautama's dates are 536–476). She has found wisdom in the Buddha's discourses and come to believe that supporting his community would be the best of benefactions. The cultural context of her time allows her to assume that her

benefactions would improve her karma and prepare her for enlightenment and nirvana (release from samsaric bondage — the
Buddhist equivalent of the Hindu *moksha*). But this motivation
is not primary. Primary is her having perceived a need that the
members of the order, men and women both, were experiencing
and thinking that she could meet it. The need is for practical
support: clothing, food, medicine, bathing cloths. (I have been
unable to find the meaning of "conjey" in any of my dictionaries
or Buddhist reference works. Perhaps it is a variant of ghee —
clarified butter or vegetable fats, a staple of the Indian diet.) As
the text unfolds, it appears that Visakha has been scandalized that
monks and nuns have sometimes gone naked for want of proper
clothing. Indeed, nuns have been embarrassed by having to bathe
at the river with prostitutes, who mocked them. Visakha wants
to help set things right. The Lord is impressed by her offer and
grants her the boon of serving the order.

If we back up slightly, we note that Gautama came on the
Indian scene as a reformer of the prevailing Indian religious cus-
toms. Not finding answers to his burning questions about the
meaning of life (how to take away the suffering caused by death,
disease, and old age), he left traditional Indian teachers (ascetical
meditation masters) and struck out on his own. By determina-
tion, he won a great victory, gaining the realization that all of life
is suffering, that the cause of suffering is desire, that if one can
uproot desire one can remove suffering, and that a program (the
Noble Eightfold Path) of meditation, morality, and wisdom can
organize one's efforts to uproot desire. This was the gist of the
Buddha's preaching, and the order arose as the ideal context in
which to put it into practice. Laypeople could certainly benefit
from hearing the Buddha's message and taking it to heart, but
the poverty, celibacy, obedience, silence, and other features of the
monastic way of life greatly facilitated Buddhist disciplehood.

Thus it happened that Buddhism became a two-track religion,
with monks and nuns occupying the inside track and laypeople
living outside the core. When a person made the profession of
faith that constituted formal admission to the ranks of the Buddha's followers, he or she professed dependence on the Buddha,
the Dharma (his Teaching), and the Sangha (his order or com-

munity, of which the monastic groups were the inner core). The monastic groups exemplified the Middle Way as lived single-mindedly. They also served laypeople as teachers and counselors. Laypeople had the obligation and privilege of supporting the monks and nuns. As the Buddha first prescribed for it, monastic life was to depend on begging. In later Buddhist history (as in Christian history) monastic groups sometimes became very wealthy and aroused considerable envy, but originally the lifestyle was supposed to be plain and poor, to facilitate wholehearted concentration on the one thing necessary: gaining enlightenment, on the model of Gautama himself.

The text does not tell us whether Visakha was married or single, old or young. It implies that she was not free to enter the monastic life herself, most likely because of temporal responsibilities. She must have been a relatively free agent, capable of disposing of her wealth as she saw fit. And she probably had the combination of a good heart and a practical intelligence honed by years of running a household or similar worldly enterprises. At any rate, we get the impression that she saw a need and immediately determined to meet it. Whether she was amused or offended at the impracticality of the monks and nuns, which had led them to put up with what she considered intolerable physical conditions, we cannot say. The bias of laypeople tends to be that professional contemplatives sometimes don't know enough to come in out of the rain (rather literally so, in this text). For their part, professional contemplatives tend to think that laypeople make far too much of material, worldly considerations and so neglect their spiritual development. In Buddhism, as in Christianity, the ideal has been for the two vocations to overlap and provide one another checks and balances.

Later Buddhist developments upgraded the place of the layperson and suggested that those living in the world suffered no disadvantage when it came to gaining enlightenment. These developments are often associated with Mahayana Buddhism, the version that did best in East Asia (China, Japan, Korea, Vietnam). Mahayana became more interested in the heavenly (divine) Buddha than in the human Buddha Gautama, so Theravadin texts usually have a more historical flavor (though they too are greatly idealized). At any rate, we see Gautama blessing the instincts of Visakha, and by doing so placing his stamp of approval on something stereotypically feminine.

For in most cultures through the ages it has been women who have tended to the practical affairs of religious groups. Prepared by caring for children, serving meals, nursing the sick, and the like, women of means regularly became major supporters of leading teachers. So, for example, Martha and the other women suggested by the New Testament accounts of Jesus' ministry were the key sources of material support. They opened their homes to the disciples, much as Visakha opened her heart to the monks and nuns. Certainly many laymen have been benefactors of the main religious traditions through the centuries, but women of means tended to have more leisure, and perhaps also more need to find a cause justifying their lives. The women may also have been primed by their cultures to leave the spiritual (more prestigious) matters to men and make their contribution on the humbler level of material support.

Sometimes present-day American feminists get into hot debates about the desirability of volunteer work. The pros and cons are clear: can volunteers ever be taken fully seriously? Won't they always be perceived as amateurs and so have little status? It makes sense to argue this kind of question through, so as to clarify its implications for women's advance to full cultural equality with men. On the other hand, if such arguing means abandoning good charitable works, one has to lament the losses it can entail. What I like about Visakha is that she went right to the crux and told the Buddha what needed to be done. She described a significant problem and, in the person of herself and her resources, presented a solution. She was more interested, it seems, in getting something done than in arguing about who would get credit for it. The text suggests that the Lord knew full well the worth of what she was offering and rewarded her with both his permission and his gratitude. Ideally, all people doing good work would receive such proper acknowledgement. But the best of laypeople offer their support with little concern for whether they will be applauded. In that way, they manifest a detachment quite like the relinquishment of desire that Gautama made the key to overcoming suffering.

~ ~ ~

If, Ananda, women had not retired from household life to the homeless one, under the Doctrine and Discipline announced by The Tathagata, religion, Ananda, would long endure; a thousand years would the Good Doctrine abide. But since, Ananda, women have now retired from household life to the homeless one, under the Doctrine and Discipline announced by The Tathagata, not long, Ananda, will religion endure; but five hundred years, Ananda, will the Good Doctrine abide.[2]

—Culla-Vagga 10:1

This text suggests the ambiguous status that even the most pious Buddhist women have generally endured. The background is the view that the Buddha originally admitted only men into his order. Women could be laypeople, but they could not live the monastic life (as nuns). However, the Buddha's aunt, known as the Maha-Pajapati, was greatly taken with his teaching and begged to be admitted into the monastery. Again and again she begged, but each time he replied that women should not give up the status of householder (layperson). Discouraged, his aunt went away sad.

Soon, however, she realized that she had to keep trying. So she put on the garb of a penitent and traveled to where her nephew had wandered. There the Buddha's favorite disciple, Ananda, saw her looking woeful and learned about her heart's desire. He interceded on her behalf, but initially he had no more success than she had had on her own. Finally, Ananda tried another route. If it were not enough to remind Gautama of everything that the Maha-Pajapati had done for him while he was a child, perhaps logic could win the day. Posing a hypothetical case, he got the Buddha to admit that, if they did retire to the monastic life, women could gain the same success as men. From that admission it was only a small step to getting Gautama to agree to admit his aunt.

However, as our text makes clear, the Buddha supposedly agreed to this step reluctantly. With the admission of women, the golden age when his doctrine would flourish would be cut in half. Scholars debate whether this text represents the Buddha's own judgment or is an interpolation from a later period, when the general Indian suspicion of the virtue of women had infected Buddhism. As it stands, there is no clear explanation of why, if women are competent, their admission to the order should bring a religious decline.

Several lines of reflection wave out from this text. First, there was the notion, strong in Indian society and many other traditional societies, that women's place was in the home. Were women to move out of their place (out of the control of men), social order would probably decline. Women were so fully identified with begetting children and serving men that a monastic option, allowing women decisive say over their vocation, could seem very dangerous. Indeed, when Buddhism moved to China, where the place of women was even more circumscribed than it was in India, nunneries regularly became targets for abuse. Chinese men were furious that women should have an option to arranged marriages, childrearing, and domestic service.

Our verses do not provide the conditions that the Buddha attached to the admission of women. Only on the stipulation that she would observe eight precepts not binding on monks could his aunt begin the monastic life for women. Summarily, the eight conditions greatly subordinated nuns to monks, requiring that the oldest female bow to any male, however young; that a monk always be in the neighborhood of a nunnery, to offer guidance; and that in various key ways the religious lives of nuns be under the control of monks.

So this text presents the Buddha's admission of women into the monastic order as grudging. In Mahayana Buddhism women could symbolize sainthood (Bodhisattvahood), perhaps because East Asian cultures generally preferred a maternal face for their deities. In the Theravadin tradition from which these verses come, saints played a more restrained role and practical matters such as who controlled the monasteries and nunneries were very important.

The upshot, then, is that although women lack none of the essentials for complete success in Buddhist striving, one should treat them cautiously. Like other monastic traditions, the Buddhist sometimes became puritanical about sex. On those occasions, the standard texts, written from a male point of view, presented women as temptations — threats to male chastity. In later periods, and in some traditions nowadays, women have made quantum leaps toward equality. In several Zen groups women can head monasteries, and leading gurus have even given the opinion that women can be more open to enlightenment than men, because regularly they have less pride. The history of Mahayana Buddhism is full of stories (most rather mythological) about female saints and queens, somewhat redressing the imbalance suggested by our verses. But, if only because the cultures into which Buddhism moved were strongly patriarchal, women always had to row upstream. As in Christian monasticism, the price of their living intense religious lives could be their need to renounce anything distinctively feminine. For the overriding suspicion was that female humanity was secondary or lesser than male and so was dubious or even dangerous on its own.

For present-day American feminists, this text will offer little that is new. Again and again, both in the past and nowadays, women have experienced considerable distrust. Many women have internalized this distrust and so are suspicious of other women. But we should not miss the particular pathos of this text. If women can never find a symbolism that affirms that they are as good as men, how can they believe that it is a fine thing to be born female? In some parts of ancient Indian culture, the birth of a little girl could be announced with the words, "Nothing was born." Girls were at best a consolation prize, at worst a great burden. One would think that the deepest insights of the major world religions would overcome this sexism, and indeed they do. But all groups have held their deepest insights in fragile vessels. The cultural containers that the insights had to use were so formed by patriarchal thinking that with time the insights grew more superficial and the radical freedom of the great founder was partially lost. That happened in the first Christian generations, as we see when we study why the Pauline insight (Galatians 3:28) that in Christ there is neither male nor female never produced a social or cultural equality for women.

Something similar happened early in Buddhism. Of itself, the experience that made Gautama the Buddha (Enlightened One) had little to do with sex. It was matter of spiritual liberation, something responding to the radical problem of pervasive human suffering. Women suffered from the human condition as much as men. They died, became sick, aged. Indeed, they suffered more injustices than men and had fewer opportunities for pleasure or taking pride in their accomplishments. That their equality in suffering did not translate into a clean, thoroughgoing statement about their equality in the Buddhist community witnesses to the loss of a fine opportunity.

Women need to know, in their marrow, that God (ultimate reality) is not a sexist. If God is as unjust as the cultures in which women live, then life has no redeeming rationale. In search of a non-sexist deity, numerous women have moved to worship of a Great Goddess. Whether they do this by concentrating on minor keys of the theology of the main traditions or by becoming witches, such women are admirable for having acted on their intuition that somewhere, somehow, they have to find a justice and love that bless their humanity as fully good.

~ ~ ~

The story is that a certain woman had married into a family of rank, but had quarreled with her husband, and, decked and ornamented, until she looked like a goddess, had issued forth from Anuradhapura, early in the morning, and was returning home to her family. On her way she met the elder [Maha-Tissa], as he was on his way from Mt. Cetiya to go on his begging-rounds in Anuradhapura. And no sooner had she seen him, than the perversity of her nature caused her to laugh loudly. The elder looked up inquiringly, and observing her teeth, realized the impurity of the body, and attained to saintship.[3]

—Visuddhi-Magga, 1

This text speaks volumes about the negative associations between women and the body. First, from the outset the woman is presented unsympathetically. For an Indian woman to quarrel with her husband implied that she was lacking in proper docility. For her to paint herself up went against the Buddhist grain. It was worse than mere vanity, because it advertised that the woman was out for adventure. Neither of these two prejudgments need have been true, of course. Her husband might have been treating the woman badly, and she might have made herself up to bolster her spirits.

Second, the worst of the woman's offenses, and the one that for our text makes her behavior indefensible, was her loud laughter. This was certainly crude, granted the respect that an elder ought to receive and the quiet that a refined woman would exhibit. It probably was also lewd, in the sense of being common to the point of lasciviousness. The monk was startled into looking up (he would have been lost in meditation, guarding his senses against distraction). But how knowingly did the woman offend him?

Third, the woman's laughter and appearance stimulated the elder's enlightenment. Being struck by the woman's teeth, which reminded him of a skeleton (teeth and bones are all that survive death), the elder appreciated (for the first time) the impurity of the flesh. To concern oneself with the superficial beauty of a painted woman, as so many men did, was to involve oneself deeply in karmic bondage. Sexual desire was one of the strongest fetters. So in his purity the monk broke through the last veils separating him from full freedom and established his being beyond the reach of sensuality.

In the conclusion to the story, the woman's husband comes along, looking for her. When he asks the monk, respectfully enough, whether he has seen a woman, the monk says that something passed that way, whether man or woman he does not know. He only knows that a set of bones is walking along this road. The point is clear: all flesh is but grass (as the Bible has put it). If one looks below the surface, human beings are short-lived and will soon be food for worms. To put any stock in pleasures of the flesh is great folly. Bodily beauty is only skin deep.

Beauty of spirit can bring one to nirvana, the state of complete fulfillment.

Buddhist meditation masters such as Buddhaghosa tried to drive this point home by lurid descriptions of how the body would decay when placed in the grave, or how the bodily processes of digestion and elimination reveal its foulness. They suggest that early Buddhism harbored a somewhat Manichean streak. The body, the flesh, the world — all were filled with impurity. Only the mind, the spirit, the Teaching could be trusted. So, many Buddhist exercises have proceeded under the assumption that the more one could lessen sensuality, the better one's chances of advancing toward enlightenment would be. The idea was to purify consciousness of sensual desire — to make it a more limpid medium for perceiving the true nature of reality.

Now, other strains of Buddhism counterbalanced the dangers of Manichean or Puritanical thought. Gautama's Middle Way was a deliberate effort to strike a balance between indulgence and excessive asceticism. The story of Gautama's passage to enlightenment begins with his pampered life as a prince. When he moves out of the palace (leaving a wife and son) to find an answer to the problem of suffering that is depressing his spirit, he tries an extreme asceticism. As one of the texts puts it, when he patted his stomach he could touch his backbone. Buddhist iconography has preserved this image, regularly depicting Gautama as a haggard near-skeleton. However, Gautama finally realized that the body has to be strong and healthy, if it is to serve the spirit well. So he broke his rigorous fast, accepted nourishment, and finally gained full serenity. When he began to teach the Middle Way, he prescribed a strict but tolerable regime, with enough food, rest, and enjoyment to keep the spirit in fighting trim.

Mahayana Buddhism developed the notion that everything is intrinsically pure. Seen without the distortions of desire, the body, the natural world, and everything else in creation is filled with Buddhanature (enlightenment, intelligibility, correlation with mind). Thus anything can trigger enlightenment, and rituals such as the tea ceremony, floral arrangement, rock gardening, the martial arts, and pottery-making could become Buddhist disciplines (especially in Japan).

Nonetheless, inasmuch as Buddhists consulted the oldest canonical texts, the flesh remained suspect. This was especially true of the flesh of women. In making that judgment, Buddhists were joining many other traditional peoples who considered women more fleshly than men. Perhaps because of their involvement in the very bodily business of giving birth and nursing, women everywhere have been considered the more sensual or natural sex. Inasmuch as a group distinguished between nature and culture, it tended to associate women with nature and men with culture. Men dominated the "upper" regions: education, government, law, religion, art, science, and spiritual advancement. They considered themselves more apt for the works that transcended nature and constituted precisely human attainments. Women tended to be bogged down in practical matters, bodily affairs. To be sure, many men wanted women to concern themselves with rearing children, serving meals, and adorning themselves beautifully. Even when they were doing their husbands' bidding, though, women were taxed with being worldly, carnal, and superficial.

It is hard to overestimate the impact that this has made on both the sexes. If we put things in a contemporary American context, we can see that our Puritan heritage continues to pay dubious dividends in our inability to find a golden mean concerning the body, sex, or the value of this-worldly things. Despite a generation's worth of sexual liberation, both repression and promiscuity now dull a great many lives. We treat sex mythologically, projecting in our advertising images of love goddesses and gods. On the other hand, we deal with such matters as sex education squeamishly. In broader perspective, we are rampantly materialistic, yet we seldom become sacramental — able to see beautiful things of either nature or human production as metaphors for ultimate reality. Many of our people do not love themselves, especially their bodies. The diet, exercise, and counseling industries live off this lack of self-love.

So, we had better get our minds clear about the necessity of a religious outlook, a way of engaging with holy, ultimate reality, that enables us to love our flesh both fiercely and with detachment. Relatedly, we had better find ways to sweep the vestiges

of Puritanism from our imaginations and hearts when it comes
to the bodies of women. Women have to feel good about both
themselves and men, but that feeling good has to be more profound than what the narcissistic ads for hair conditioners offer.
Until we root our judgments about the goodness of the world
in a contemplative experience of how the world issues from the
divine goodness, we shall always be vulnerable to imbalances. I
like to think that, once enlightened, the elder Maha-Tissa praised
the beauty of the foolish woman who had laughed at him and
felt great compassion for her. For, as truly enlightened, he was
bound to see that she had been a victim of much malformation
and prejudice.

~   ~   ~

Homage to the Lady Prajnaparamita, whose virtue is immor-
tality, who responds to loving devotion, who is replete with the
knowledge of the Tathagatas, who is loving towards all.[4]
                                                    —Sadhanamala

This text comes from Mahayana circles and reflects considerable
development of the notion of wisdom (*prajna*). Here the Wisdom
that has gone beyond all worldly limitations (*Prajnaparamita*) is
addressed as a goddess. She is not the object of an academic pursuit of ultimate knowledge but the object of a prayerful petition.
Those seeking to know and enjoy her have to approach with the
trust of disciples. The verses we find here are typical of intro-
ductions to sutras falling into the Mahayana genre known as the
Prajnaparamita literature. Our verses compose a mantra, a collection of sacred sounds that the devout meditator would chant to
the Lovely Lady. Notice that her strength or righteousness makes
her deathless, that she is glad when people petition her lovingly,
that she possesses all the wisdom of enlightenment (the Tathagatas are Buddhas — those who have realized "suchness": how
things actually are), and that she regards all beings with love.

Two things are worth reflection. First, notice the prominence
of love in the profile of the Lady Wisdom. For Buddhism, the ul-

timate wisdom that discloses how reality actually is constituted is shot through with *mahakaruna* — great compassion. When Gautama perceived the state of most human beings, he was moved by his compassion to preach the Way. When a bodhisattva (saint or Buddha-to-be) reached the threshold of nirvana, he or she would hold back, in order to labor for the salvation of all living things — out of great compassion. On the whole, Buddhist love is less emotional than Western love, because it wants to avoid desire. Desire is the trap, the fault keeping people chained to the karmic realm (*samsara:* the realm of deaths and rebirths). But the sweet reason of the Lady Prajnaparamita is tender-hearted. Although she moves beyond desire, she listens to those who approach her and works for their good.

Second, Wisdom is feminine. If one has to picture how the ultimate insight appears, one ought to make it lovely, gracious, subtle, attractive, and kind like a woman. Buddhism had enough thinkers who denied the validity of the human imagination in the realm of ultimate reality to safeguard it against idolatry. On the other hand, many Buddhists realized that to be fully effective teachings about ultimate reality had to take on forms that encouraged holistic contemplation. Wisdom had to become something or someone to whom the faithful could pray, whom they could praise and petition. In the case of the Prajnaparamita literature, the highest speculation melded with a devotion reinforced by the use of mantras.

The text that we have could be enhanced by a mandala — a collection of sacred sights. In the source from which we have taken this text, the example given of an appropriate mandala is an eight-petaled lotus. The lotus is the traditional symbol of Buddhist victory: beauty (truth, wisdom) rising up from the muck of worldliness. So in a typical Prajnaparamita meditation one might correlate one's chanting to the Lady Wisdom with a progressive visualization of the different petals of the lotus. The result intended would be a whole-hearted engagement with the beauty of wisdom, and so a renewed dedication to pursuing it. As well, the result ideally would be a deeper appreciation of the subtle, gentle, fertile way that wisdom operates in the mind and throughout the world.

We may recall that other religious cultures have also represented ultimate wisdom as feminine. As we shall see, the Tao
that ancient China considered the pathway to both social order
and personal peace carried more feminine overtones than male.
In biblical writings such as Proverbs and Wisdom, a feminine
principle played alongside God when he ordered the universe.
Called Lady Wisdom (Hokhma), she could appear like a gracious
housewife, laying a table for all the hungry, calling all the simple
to leave their stupidity and profit from her offer.

When it comes to making ultimate wisdom something whole,
the associations of women with nourishment, grace, beauty, gen-
tleness, fertility, and subtlety seem to have determined that feminine figures would prevail. This is interesting for several reasons.
First, it can give women's ways of knowing a boost, suggesting
that the intelligence running the universe is subtle and whole
rather than obvious and linear. Second, it can suggest that the
logic assumed to be proper for running worldly things, when
men prevail, is not adequate when it comes to ultimate things.
Third, it can support a fusion of knowing and loving in the depths
of creativity. And, fourth, it can explain why Buddhism has always found enlightenment to move people toward compassion.
When they have passed beyond this-worldly perspectives and limitations, the great saints have found their hearts opening to all
creatures. Now able to perceive how much suffering there is in
the world, the great saints sympathize deeply with those still in
bondage and do their best to help them. The Lady Prajnaparamita
is the inspiration of such saints, glad to be petitioned and loving
in all her responses.

Few who are not contemplatives will take much pleasure in ru-
minating about the images of Lady Wisdom or speculating about
her significance. Unless one is used to nourishing one's soul on
metaphors for ultimate reality (even metaphors that lead one into
darkness), reading about them, let alone chanting or visualizing
them, will have little appeal. And yet most of us have drawn spiritual nourishment or refreshment from literature, films, paintings,
or symphonies. Images from the Bible and Shakespeare were the
wellspring of Western culture for hundreds of years. So if we suffer an atrophy of our capacity to wonder about metaphors for

God, we are much to be pitied. The Buddhists who venerated Lady Wisdom knew the great extent to which she was a creation of their own minds. They were well aware that she was only a useful fiction. But they also knew that by chanting to her they could compose their souls in peace and give their minds pictures conducive to enlightenment.

The human spirit has a natural hunger for wisdom. To know the ultimate order of things is part of the desire built into our minds and hearts. We are restless until we can contemplate a cause, a reason, a beauty that makes sense of all our experience. We seek something or someone to love exhaustively — someone or something as vast and good as our hearts' fullest desires postulate. The Buddhist twist on this Western (Augustinian) analysis of the natural human desire for God is detachment. When one comes into the presence of Lady Wisdom, the grasping that keeps people in karmic bondage falls away. Because one's beloved is present, there is no need to be restless. What one lacked and so strove to gain is at hand. So what we might call a lofty complacency overbalances the concern and agitation that drove one prior to contemplative union.

The implication for present-day Americans is clear. If we are long on desirous striving and short on complacent (from the Latin *complacentia* — taking pleasure with) appreciation, we are going to miss the implications of Wisdom and not realize her many presences in our midst. The Buddhist can consider her to be the reason or guide illumining all situations. In every time and place she can draw near to repeat the lesson that the things we pursue are empty and can never give us full satisfaction. Only when we pry our hands loose and let things reveal themselves to be tokens of the ultimate mystery of existence will we perceive correctly and gain full peace. When they chanted to Lady Wisdom, Mahayana Buddhists let their spirits be moved by her imagery to a light-fingered love of creation. Caressing rather than grasping, appreciating rather than trying to use, the contemplative spirit of the Prajnaparamita tells us volumes about the ideal interactions with reality. Only when we are detached and loving will reality be able to reveal its full beauty to us.

Now further, Ananda, there appeared to the King of Glory the Woman-Treasure, graceful in figure, beautiful in appearance, charming in manner, and of the most fine complexion; neither very tall, nor very short; neither very stout, nor very slim; neither very dark, nor very fair; surpassing human beauty, she had attained unto the beauty of the gods. The touch too, Ananda, of the skin of that wondrous Woman was as the touch of cotton or of cotton wool: in the cold her limbs were warm, in the heat her limbs were cool; while from her body was wafted the perfume of sandal wood and from her mouth the perfume of the lotus.[5]*
—Maha-Sudassana 1:36–37*

The context is a speech of the Buddha to his favorite disciple about the fabled king who used to rule the place where they have stopped. Ananda is afraid that the Buddha will die in what he takes to be a backwater town, but the Buddha assures him that the town has a fine lineage. In detailing the glories and achievements of its fabled king, the Buddha comes to the king's consort, the idealized woman. The first verses describing her deal with her physical appearance.

This description is sensuous without being sensual. Her beauty is more the perfection of feminine potential than a loveliness exciting desire. Moreover, it is a beauty that is retiring rather than aggressive. The woman takes no special care about her appearance. She simply is graceful, charming, and the rest, apparently unselfconsciously. This suggests that the Buddhist ideal of beauty fit the sense of harmony and peace that the Middle Way sought. True beauty was an overflow of virtuous being. The woman who accosted the elder on the road, laughing crudely, was not beautiful. No matter how skillful her self-adornment, how dazzling her smile, the elder saw only a collection of bones. The beauty of the Woman-Treasure complements the reality of human existence instead of trying to disguise it. The grace and charm of the king's consort overflowed from her good spirit and suggested how virtue could defeat the grave. Her wonderful complexion would not last forever, but it revealed a perfect harmony at the center of her being that would prove more powerful than her mortality.

In her perfection, the woman avoided all extremes. She was average in size, rather than exceptionally large or small, so she did not put any observer off. The implication is that she was just what a woman ought to be — extraordinarily ordinary. This was the tip-off to her special status, her beauty like that of a goddess. The text stresses the softness of the woman's touch, the perfect temperature of her limbs, and the good smells that came out of her. Yet even these sensuous details carry little erotic charge. The woman is desirable as a consort, but sexual use of her is not to the fore. The tone is more one of admiration and giving objective beauty its due than of taking sexual pleasure.

A text such as this requires us to place further nuance on our impressions of early Buddhism. Many early texts are ascetical and present matters of the flesh negatively. They depict women as more problematic than helpful, and they seem to cast a pall over ordinary life. Preoccupied with how to escape from life's sufferings, they underscore the fleetingness of earthly life and the imperative character of the call to snuff out desire. This text is more at home in the world and with the body. It associates physical beauty with high human achievement. The King of Glory was the ideal monarch, and it was only fitting that his consort should be beautiful. Did this sketch of ideal femininity compromise Buddhism's message to women and complicate how they were inclined to think about themselves?

It must have, to some extent. For no earthly woman could live up to the sketch of beauty we find here, and every earthly woman delighted by the message that the key to life was gaining enlightenment must have wondered whether she wasn't being forced back into the game of making herself physically beautiful. How complete was the liberation of her spirit, if in fact enlightenment wasn't the whole story and being physically beautiful remained important?

On the other hand, some women might have felt that beauty should remain part of the ideal. Thinking that loving beauty, whether in nature or other people, was a natural and healthy response, such women might have cheered this challenge to the dour aspects of the early tradition, glad to move from a rejection of the flesh to a balanced appreciation. As long as this appreciation did not become driven by desire, but remained objective and un-grasping, it could seem saner, healthier, than the fears spotlighted by the monks' psychology.

This complicated reaction to the question of beauty epitomizes the burden that women have carried in most cultures. Women have been the beautiful sex, the prime representatives of fine form and grace as well as wisdom. Indeed, it is difficult to separate the place of beauty from the place of sweet reason in the profile of Lady Wisdom. Her physical grace is a sacramental expression of her knowledge of ultimate mysteries. Because the canonical texts have been written by men, women have appeared as both more beautiful and more dangerous (morally ugly) than men. Women have been the abnormal, the extreme, while men have been the normal. Men might be handsome, but it was more important that they be intelligent, strong, and disciplined. Women would ideally be disciplined, but most cultures thought that women required the control of men to gain such discipline. The goddess could be an exception, but even the Indian (Hindu) goddesses could be depicted as running amok without the control of their consorts.

When women speak up for themselves rather than taking their self-images from patriarchal texts, they tend to seek a balanced view of wisdom and beauty. On the one hand, they want to de-velop ideals of human success that make goodness, intelligence, virtue, and similarly spiritual attainments the crux. These are open to women and men equally, and when they rule definitions of human success, women enjoy an equal share of truly human op-portunity. On the other hand, women want to be fully human precisely as women. They do not want to forfeit their sexuality, because that is an inalienable part of their identity. They do not want to have their beauty defined by outsiders, any more than they want to have their virtue defined by outsiders, because that is alienating. So the sort of beauty they praise is not the sort pro-moted by the advertising industry, which manipulates women constantly in view of male pleasure. A better sort of beauty is one that gives the female body and spirit their due — one that promotes grace, health, charm, proportion, and the like without regard to the measurements of pin-up girls.

All of this remains rather ideal, however, because women have to work out their views of beauty and virtue in the midst of cultures seriously tainted by desire. Men's desire for women as objects of pleasure, and women's desire to be beautiful according to male standards, collude to distort the whole question of an ideal feminine beauty. Little in the ideal sketched in our text is offensive, except the entire premise that the Woman-Treasure is mainly an adornment of the King of Glory. The text is not lewd or exploitative physically, but it comes from a patriarchal culture that makes women's pleasing men their primary reason to be. This suggests how deeply any religion, even one as radical as Buddhism, is embedded in its time and culture. For both women and men, the development of an independent standard of beauty is a sign of great religious liberation and maturity.

~ ~ ~

That Pearl among Women too, Ananda, used to rise up before the Great King of Glory, and after him retire to rest; pleasant was she in speech, and ever on the watch to hear what she might do in order so to act as to give him pleasure. That Pearl among Women too, Ananda, was never, even in thought, unfaithful to the Great King of Glory — how much less could she be so with the body![6]

—Maha-Sudassana 1:38–39

These verses complete the description of the Woman-Treasure, the feminine ideal befitting the King of Glory. Here the focus is not the woman's physical beauty but her complete dedication to her Lord. The description is stereotypically Indian to the point of amusement. The woman exists only to please her Lord. She has no life of her own, apart from this function. All of her energy is devoted to anticipating his next need or pleasure and fulfilling it. Of course it is unthinkable that she would ever be unfaithful to him. We see, then, that Buddhism took over the concern for women's obedience and purity that preoccupied Indian culture (and Muslim culture, and most other patriarchal cultures). Obviously, this ideal stems from a time so distant from our own (morally more than physically) that we must strain to understand it. Even when we do strain, we can feel that we ought not to — that by mustering sympathy and gaining understanding we are corrupting ourselves.

To my mind, the only way to redeem a passage such as this is to find a parallel one in which the male would be as dedicated to the female. Finding that, we could think that the culture in question had achieved justice between the sexes by a different route than our contemporary feminist ones. In its own way, that other culture would have honored the intuition that women and men are equally human. The problem is, we seldom find such parallel texts in patriarchal cultures. The spirit and content of the text we have here are quite representative. Women have been made to serve men, and the ideal woman is dedicated completely to the needs and pleasures of her husband. Sometimes her brief is expanded to include the needs of her entire family (which only increases her burdens), but almost never does it grant her the right, let alone the responsibility, to look after her own needs as well. In the most logical and thoroughgoing cases, the argument becomes that women's nature is to serve others and so their fulfillment lies in self-abnegation. The convenience in this definition seems to escape most of the male authority figures who propose it.

When set against this background, the counsels of contemporary feminist psychology become more intelligible. Those counsels often boil down to the need for women to include themselves prominently among the people upon whom they expend care. This need sometimes explodes in women who have spent most of their lives serving others and feel they have come up empty or been jobbed. Because they did not care for themselves, they ran out of strength to serve others. Few men fit this stereotype. Most men have learned through their social conditioning that it is completely legitimate to take time off, find pleasurable hobbies, and measure their self-spending against their resources.

Even though the truth of this counsel from feminist psychology may seem obvious, several factors militate against women's accepting it. The first and most powerful is the weight of patriarchal history and culture, which has schooled most women to think of themselves as called to nurture others. Second, and related, is the investment in this self-image that many women have made by middle age. If it turns out that the image is dysfunctional, a woman may have to reevaluate her entire life, which of course is very painful. Third, there is the fact that some women are selfish or narcissistic (as some men are), that these are unattractive traits, and so that preaching self-love can clash on sensitive ears. Then the trick is to make it clear that a proper self-love is manifested most dramatically in the way that it frees people from wrongful self-concern.

My sense is that most of the secular foundations offered for self-love are superficial and therefore encourage narcissism. The woman mouthing "I'm worth it" as she plops down her charge card is a victim of false advertising, and more times than not she doesn't really believe what she's mouthing. Her attention to herself is a desperate effort to convince a doubting conscience, and because it is a scam it never succeeds. The great religions speak of a more universal love that can stabilize any person, man or woman, in a proper self-esteem, one that is convincing because it does not come from the fallible self but from the Creator or ultimate reality that cannot fail.

Sometimes one hears the objection that people cannot derive their worth from anything outside themselves, because if they do they don't own their own goodness — their self-love will not be authentic. This objection fails in the case of a true divinity or ultimate reality, because it misses the unique nature of the relationship between the Creator and the creature. Seen properly, this relationship is such that the creature becomes more herself the more closely she is united with the Creator. God is not a competitor, working against the self's best interests. The more that creatures try to isolate themselves from their Creator, thinking that autonomy would be maturity, the more they frustrate their development and happiness. In fact, we find ourselves only in the mystery of existence. The more deeply we participate in the mystery of existence, the more our uniqueness and fulfillment emerge.

The Buddhist variations on this general religious thesis are interesting, because a fundamental axiom of Buddhist analysis has it that there is no self. This does not mean that Buddhists do not recognize the differences between Mary and every other creature in the world. It does not mean that Mary is not unique. It means that Mary finds her full identity only outside herself, in the context of the whole of reality, especially the depth called nirvana. Mary, like all other beings, is "empty" in her "own-being." She does not explain herself. She cannot fulfill herself. She becomes enlightened, luminous to herself, only when she realizes that nothing (no-thing) in existence is her foundation. She depends on the mystery of being, which is a reality of a different order from anything created. When she realizes this, so that her dependence is voluntary and free, she opens herself to the richest measures of self-love and creativity.

The problem with the world religions' insights into this crucial matter of the foundations of self-love and creativity has been their failure to develop the social consequences. Primary among these social consequences ought to be the equality of women and men, based on their equally complete dependence on God or ultimate reality (Nirvana, Suchness, the Buddhanature). The many texts such as this present one about the ideal woman have vitiated much of the message. Women have learned the part about self-spending (which becomes possible when one is held by the divine love), but often they have not learned the part about the self-love that divinity inculcates. Men have learned the part about self-love, but often they have not learned the part about self-spending, especially as regards women. The better message would be that both men and women depend completely on divinity for their being and worth, that this is liberating, that from it should flow a healthy self-love, and that loving others as one loves oneself (taking care, being willing to sacrifice, not being willing to ruin oneself) is not difficult when one feels well-treated.

The ideal woman in our text gives no sign of feeling ill-treated, but we all know that many women have been ill-treated throughout history. Indeed, the feminists among us believe that patriarchy is by definition ill-treatment, because it denies the crucial truth that the sexes ought to love themselves and serve one another as equals. Women are not made simply to serve men, and men are not made simply to serve women. Both sexes are made to love themselves and one another in a great circle of affirmation initiated and sustained by God.

4

Chinese Texts

The Master said, "I suppose I should give up hope. I have yet to meet the man who is as fond of virtue as he is of beauty in women."[1]

—Analects 15:13

The Master is Confucius (551–479 B.C.E.), the great teacher of traditional China. The Analects collect sayings attributed to him. Usually the context is discussions with his favorite disciples. None of those disciples was a woman, and women figured very little in the discussions. That in itself speaks eloquently about the secondary status of women in traditional Chinese culture. Women were to obey men and give them children. If affection ruled between the sexes, so much the better. But first came service and fertility. In this text we find a hint of the reason why the Master disregarded women. They could be a hindrance to the pursuit of virtue that was the hallmark of the gentlemen Confucius was trying to develop.

Such virtue expressed itself through set social relationships, all of them hierarchical. First, children were to obey their parents and serve them. Filial piety was the foundation of traditional Chinese culture and veneration for the elderly extended filial piety. Ancient China was a very conservative culture, much concerned to live by the models passed down from the golden ages of the distant past. Confucius described himself as a conservator rather than an innovator. He wanted his teaching to be a great act of homage to the heroes of yore, the ancients whose Way was the people's best hope for living harmoniously with nature and in

89

society. So Confucius looked backward and emphasized following traditional authorities. The only thing revolutionary about his teaching, when one compared it with the mores of his day, was his insistence that solid rule stemmed from virtue rather than force or guile.

The second great social relationship was between men and women. Simply and exhaustively, men were superior and women inferior. Confucius disregarded any potential women might have to live as the equals of men, let alone as men's superiors. The only care for women that the Analects records the Master taking was to find good husbands for the women in his charge. There is no mention of his own wife and no discussion of relations between husbands and wives.

The other key social relations included rulers and subjects, elder brothers and younger siblings, and teachers and pupils. In each case, the former were wholly the superior and the latter wholly the inferior. A well-ordered society demanded that both parties to relationships such as these play their roles conscientiously. Superiors had to bear their responsibility to rule, and inferiors had to obey promptly and fully. In the Confucian scheme of things, social order began in the family. If husbands ruled their wives and parents ruled their children, the rest of the common weal would follow. Ideally, the rule of husbands and parents would be wise, virtuous, and benevolent. Ideally, the obedience of wives and children would be full of affection and respect. But even without wisdom and affection, the relationships remained crystal clear.

Apart from their utility as mothers and servants, women tended to be more bother than they were worth. Daughters had to be safeguarded, provided a dowry, and married off. When married they left their natal family and joined their husband's. So whatever their parents expended on their behalf paid little return. It was their husband's family who profited from their talent. Moreover, and worse from Confucius's point of view, women could distract men from their most noble task, becoming fully human — gentlemen. The Confucian gentleman excelled in knowing what ought to be done and how to do it. His expertise was a blend of learning and prudence. He had to know the ancient sources and the protocol for significant social occasions. Even more, he had to know the spirit of the ancient sources and protocol — how the Way inspired them. The Master said that it took him until he was seventy before his own will and the Way coincided. Complete mastery of the traditional wisdom, complete familiarity with the Way, was the fruit of a lifetime's struggle. So any distraction from this struggle was the Master's enemy. Simply by being attractive, women could siphon off energy much better put into study. Society depended on the study of potential gentlemen. Without people learned and virtuous, it would become a shambles. Thus the attractiveness of women was a threat to the common good.

That is a somewhat negative reading of the Master's views of women, teased out of the very few texts relevant to the issue, but it was verified frequently throughout Chinese history. In most periods Confucius was the leading master, and so the misogynism of traditional Chinese culture cannot be separated from the Master's dismissal of women. I find myself amused that, despite the formidable power of Confucius's own thought and the later tradition, female charm could so easily counterbalance it.

For Chinese women naturally had their own views of their importance to their culture. Heavily indoctrinated in Confucian ethics though they were, some vestiges of pride and self-knowledge told them that much of the Master's talk was bunk. At the least, it was stuffy. At the most, it was simply untrue. Every intelligent woman burdened with a stupid father, husband, or elder brother knew that it was impossible to accept the Confucian hierarchy of relationships uncritically. Similarly, every woman who fell in love or who saw how power politics actually unfolded, knew that the virtue of supposed gentlemen was a frail reed on which to lean. Certainly women who understood the central Confucian virtue of *jen* (love, fellow-feeling, humaneness) could be gratified to find that it was holistic — a matter of heart as much as mind. But on the whole the Confucian system so looked down upon women that women were bound to hedge their loyalties to it. Only when they had carved out the domestic sphere as a zone of their own authority, or when they had bound their male children to themselves, or when they had developed the sanctioned shrewishness that mainstream culture allowed them as a safety-valve could the majority of Chinese women relate to Confucian standards as something benefiting them. Women did better as they aged, because they benefited from the veneration the elderly might expect. Even in death, however, women were second to men: the period of mourning for a mother could be shorter than that for a father.

In such a cultural context, it is amazing that Chinese women survived as well as they did. Many stories suggest that strong women ignored the subjugation officially expected of them and tested the limits, sometimes to the extent of doing what they pleased. Among the peasantry (always the great majority), women's work often was as significant as that of men, which gave the women some leverage. Among the trading classes women sometimes became the predominant businesspeople. But even many women who had few tangible props for the case that they were the equals of men refused to give the going Confucian structures full allegiance, as an act of semi-knowing resistance. Something in them knew that the Master's views of women were badly flawed, just as something in many peasants knew that being a noble did not make a person intelligent.

The bottom line in the story of women's struggles to gain adequate images of themselves is that reality finally will make its impact. There is no way that any system, no matter how patriarchal, can block out the equality of women in native intelligence or the experience of what makes for wisdom. So women have tended to reset the rules, even as they have worked within given patriarchal structures. They have tended to form enclaves in which they could gossip, satirize male authority, heal one another's wounds, and develop alternative readings of the world. It would have been beneath the dignity and interest of Confucius to bother about this feminine culture, but that was his loss. Better than half the population lived by a worldview significantly different from canonical Confucianism. No genuine master can ignore such a reality. The parallels nowadays remain clear, even though feminists have made American culture much more egalitarian than traditional Chinese culture. Women still have to articulate their own sense of how the world hangs together and how the sexes relate if the race is to have the whole fund of wisdom that it needs to survive.

~ ~ ~

> *The ceremony of marriage was intended to be a bond of love between two [families of different] surnames, with a view, in its retrospective character, to secure the services in the ancestral temple, and in its prospective character, to secure the continuance of the family line. Therefore, the superior men [the ancient rulers] set a great value upon it."* [2]
>
> —Book of Rites, chap. 44

The Book of Rites was one of Confucius's main authorities. Handed down from the pre-Confucian past, it collected much of the lore that Confucius considered canonical. Here the discussion of marriage makes it utterly clear that the principal consideration was familial rather than personal. The bride and groom were functionaries for their clans. Their parents or other elders arranged the marriage. No doubt good parents took into account the character of the spouses, to try to effect a happy union, but the first order of business was to secure the continuance of the lineage and gain good relations with a desirable external clan. That the love of the marital bond was to be between the clans (with the love of the two spouses not even mentioned) summarizes how traditional China felt.

Behind this feeling lies the further dimension of clan existence: the status of the ancestors. Ancient Chinese looked to their children for support in old age, but perhaps more important were the sacrifices the children would offer after the parents' death. That is the import of the reference to services in the ancestral temple. Retrospectively, concerning those who had gone before, it was crucially important that the couple marrying give good prospects for raising children who would be faithful in making the prescribed sacrifices. On those sacrifices depended the peace of the ancestors in the world of the departed. If no one were to sacrifice for them, or if the sacrifices were slovenly, then the ancestors could roam in discontent, appearing like ghosts to badger the living to do right by them. All the generations therefore had a large stake in a marriage. Inasmuch as the elderly dominated matters such as marriage, they saw to it that the prospective partners seemed likely to do well by both clan lines.

The prospective character of the marriage was the children one could expect. Those standing at the ceremony were the hinge between past and future. If the ancestors (going back dozens of generations) represented the past, the loins of the marital couple represented the future, which the clan hoped would stretch equally lengthily. Thus the fertility of the couple was a major matter. In practice this meant the fertility of the female much more than the male, so from the day of her marriage the bride was under pressure to conceive and bring forth healthy progeny, especially males. Since the clan lineage was reckoned through the male line, sons were the great prize. Without sons, there would be no heads of household to offer the sacrifices and the clan would acquire a secondary status, existing only along the female line. In her husband's household, the bride's lineage took second place.

The bride was supposed to be a virgin, mainly for the sake of confidence about the lineage of the children she would produce. Were the bride not a virgin, the possibility existed that her first child would not be by her husband. After marriage, the wife was supposed to be chaste, having relations only with her husband, because this too was necessary if the lineage, the sacrifices, and all the rest were to stay in good order. One has to remember that fertility, lineage, and the rest were all powerful, mythic entities in ancient cultures like the pre-Confucian Chinese. Indeed, fertility was a numinous matter — something involving divine mystery. Some of this mythology spilled over onto women, whose otherness retained at least vestiges of something awesome, even in patriarchal China. So the prospective dimension of marriage weighed especially heavily on young women. Until they had proven fertile, they had no justification. Indeed, if they proved infertile, they could be shipped back to their natal family in disgrace.

Men were not required to come to marriage as virgins, and the strictures against adultery were nowhere near so strong for men as for women. It was more accepted than not that men might frequent women not their wives, because a wife was not necessarily a friend, lover, or even partner for sexual pleasure. A wife was an approved source of children and the continuance of the clan. She had responsibilities, and so rights, within the household, and she received much counsel, and some training, in how to make herself valued. No doubt there were cases in which husbands and wives delighted in one another and made together a truly personal bond of affection. But that remained quite peripheral in the Confucian scheme of things. More than in classical India, where a code such as Manu made the honoring of women a matter of religious significance, in classical China the affection one had for women was optional. If the Analects be a faithful indication, Confucius expended much more affection and concern on his male students than on any woman in his household.

Perhaps the main lesson we should take away is how prepersonal many traditional cultures were. Only in the West, probably at the end of the Middle Ages, did the romantic notion of love that is at the heart of our present notions of personhood differentiate itself from a welter of familial concerns and become a potent factor in its own right. Without this romantic notion, prior peoples were hard pressed to make a case against the regulation of marriage in terms of family lineage. What the spouses felt for one another on their wedding day interested the sensitive, but no one would have construed the union, or the fate of the young spouses, in terms of a passion that could sear their souls with the fire that had made the world originally.

This is not to say, of course, that ancient China knew nothing about erotic love, or even about agape, the personal love that is self-sacrificing. It is just to say that such knowledge remained idiosyncratic. It did not enter the mainstream to shape the institution of marriage. It did not factor significantly in considerations of how to raise one's children or think about one's social responsibilities.

Sometimes each sex tends to consider the other romantic and argue that it has the more realistic view of love. In fact, both sexes can be romantic, in both the good and the pejorative senses of the word, and each sex needs the other if it is to be realistic about love. What is common to romantic women and men is the hope that their attraction will take them outside themselves, to the realms of beauty, creativity, and perhaps even holiness that they have glimpsed in their best dreams. Also common is the hope that they will find together a fulfillment that they could not find alone. All of this is romantic in the positive sense of being aware that sexual love, in its fully personal implications, is a force of unique experiential power.

What both sexes need if they are to be realistic includes the recognition that even the best romantic love operates within objective social patterns that it cannot remove and should not overlook. Even the best of lovers cannot cordon themselves off from the world and make a paradise all their own. So, even the best of lovers will have to endure the imperfections of the world outside them. In time, of course, they will also have to face the imperfections of their own selves. Because they live in the social world differently and have somewhat different selves, men and women best help one another become realistic by sharing their perceptions, judgments, hopes, successes, and failures. The pity of the ancient Chinese couple seen at their marriage ceremony is that so little of this precisely personal part of their adventure could be clear to them.

~ ~ ~

The spirit of the valley never dies. This is called the mysterious female. The gateway of the mysterious female is called the root of heaven and earth. Dimly visible, it seems as if it were there, yet use will never drain it.[3]

—Tao Te Ching 6/17

The traditional Chinese view has been that Lao Tzu, the reputed author of the Tao Te Ching, was an older contemporary of Confucius. A more critical view, based on textual and historical studies, suggests that Lao Tzu was not a historical figure and that the book attributed to him is more a collection of texts from the Taoist school (fourth century B.C.E.) than an original, consistent composition. At any rate, the Taoists (followers of the Tao, or Way) came to represent an alternative to Confucian orthodoxy. The slogan "In office a Confucian, in retirement a Taoist" captures some of the most important differences between the two groups. Confucianism became the state orthodoxy, because it offered a rational analysis of how social relations ought to proceed. Taoism offered more to the individual seeking to understand the mysteriousness of the human condition.

The only problem with this characterization of the two schools is that Taoism had a strong political component and Confucianism made the virtue of the individual ruler (or gentleman) its pivotal point. The "retirement" of the Taoist therefore is better understood as a contemplative distancing than as a purely private or solitary life. In the classical Chinese scheme of the life cycle, like that of classical India, it was accepted, even encouraged, that people entering upon old age take time off for reflection. The natural time in China was at the death of one's parents. That signaled one's passover from dependent to elder, and a major reason for the extended mourning period (three years was standard) was to appropriate the significance of one's mortality. Having done so, one was more likely to appreciate the traditions passed down from the immemorial past that had allowed one's people to survive generation after generation. This was all quite objective, tying into the understanding of marriage that we mentioned: the great task was to keep the family line going.

The Taoist wrinkle on this general Chinese preoccupation with family lineage, veneration for the elderly, and the like was a poetic or mystical immersion in the wonders of the Way. The Way both could and could not be expressed. Ultimately, it could not be expressed. It was too primordial for anything so derivate as a human intelligence to express it. But human beings could get a glimpse of it, or could infer some of its characteristics from its effects in the world. For our purposes, the most interesting such inferences suggested that the Tao presented itself in imagery more feminine than masculine.

Our text is a meditation on the spirit, the sense, of the Tao that works in the world, causing creation and giving human beings a hint of the standards they will follow if they are wise. The Tao is more like the valley than the mountain. The mountain stands high, is prominent, and gets worn down by the winds and rains. The valley is hidden, humble, lowly, and less troubled by storms, more likely to be a place of peace and prosperity. This spirit of survival-through-humility never dies or goes out of style. It is the way of nature itself, more times than not. For though nature can rage in storms and draw attention to itself, most of the time it works quietly, unobtrusively, accomplishing the great wonders (the seasons, the species) with little fuss.

Why is the spirit of the valley called the mysterious female? Because we can never fully comprehend it. Because it seems more akin to the stereotypical woman than the stereotypical man. And because it is fertile, a source of life generation after generation. Inasmuch as the ancient Chinese looked upon the world in wonder that it was so fertile, they thought of it as a great Mother. When the Tao, the Way, materialized itself, it gave birth to the ten thousand things of creation. So naturally it appeared to be maternal. Heaven, one of the oldest Chinese deities, carried masculine overtones, because heaven seemed to oversee everything and rule from on high. But earth had its own patterns, principles, laws, difficult though it was for human beings to grasp them. These patterns were the elusive logic of females, as they went about their natural tasks of bringing forth new life.

The gateway of the mysterious female is the connection between the Tao that cannot be named and the Tao that somewhat can. One can look for this connection in the human spirit and find that it is that fine point of the human spirit whence come our images of how the divine mystery moves through the world. Or one can look for it in external nature and find that it is the generative power of matter and the style that nature uses to shape the world day by day. Thus water wearing away rock, an infant forcing the entire household to adapt to it, a craftsperson going with the grain in wood or jade rather than against it — all exemplify the wisdom of the Tao, the sense of how the Mother has made her offspring to work.

These hinges suggest the root of heaven and earth because they are our best intuitions of the "logic" of the situation in which we find ourselves. When we ask about how divinity deals with us, how the powers of creation present themselves, we are apt to end up contemplating the strange arising of existence and meaning at the border of mystery and mind. We have the mind, though in very limited degree. The mystery is the beyond from which

light and being come. We are bound to think that the source
of existence comes from beyond us, because we are finite and
existence seems unlimited in every way (spatially, temporally, on-
tologically, morally). If it makes sense to speak about what gives
the human condition (as summarized by "heaven and earth,"
our spiritual and material reaches) its rootage, then the gateway,
the womb, of the mysterious motherly source is a sensible con-
tender for the job. Buddhist cosmology spoke of the Womb of
the Buddha (Tathagata-garba): the fullness from which existence
(suchness) emerges. Ancient Taoist thought was groping after a
similar perception.

The final verses summarize the metaphysical intuitions on
which the Tao Te Ching depends. We have just enough of a hint
about the ultimate origins of the world to allow us to speculate
about them and so answer (minimally) our spirit's ineluctable
questions. When we pay attention to this hint, we realize that the
cause of the world has to be present, if the world is to exist. The
mystery of existence is as physical, as present, as existence itself,
even though its mode of presence is too simple and basic for us
to process. With an appreciation of the presence of the mystery
that is our best "explanation" for existence comes the further insight that it is inexhaustible. It has provided the countless beings,
in their wild diversity and so many different kinds. It has always
been and shows all signs of continuing into a limitless future. It
is a plenitude, a pleroma, that will never be drained. Unlike limited things, it does not dry up with use or wear out. Its nature
seems to be to create, draw forth, share, so that production does
not diminish it. It is the original, the font, and so all wisdom has
to focus upon it. Otherwise, one would be neglecting the only
thing truly necessary.

For Chinese women, being associated with the one thing truly
necessary did not translate into social status equal to that of men.
But the Taoists did defend women against the worst of Confucian misogyny, such as encouragement of female infanticide, and
they did keep present in Chinese higher culture the perception
that true wisdom, both personal and political, has a lot of paradox about it. For example, it is like the way that gnarled trees
and women survive better than straight, desirable trees and men.

It is like the power of persuasion by which women get men to do their will (including their will to become pregnant) more than the brutal application of physical force. The Tao is feminine in being subtle, indirect, holistic. When Westerners speak of the mysterious Orient, and boggle at the indirections of Oriental cultures, they are paying homage to the femininity of the Tao.

~   ~   ~

The world had a beginning, and this beginning could be the mother of the world. When you know the mother, go on to know the child. After you have known the child, go back to holding fast to the mother, and to the end of your days you will not meet with danger.

—Tao Te Ching 52/117

This text offers us more of the obscure poetry that has made the Tao Te Ching serviceable and beloved for more than two thousand years (it is the most translated Chinese text). The world had a beginning. The Tao did not necessarily have a beginning. There was a Way before there was a world, and the world arose because the Tao manifested itself. To say that the world had a beginning is to move beyond the perceptions of common sense. For ancient Chinese science, nature changed constantly, but largely by reshuffling a few basic ingredients. The conviction that there was a beginning in a metaphysical sense is less a statement about creation in time than a statement about the dependence of the world. The world only began when the Tao, its metaphysical source and superior, granted it the forms that brought it into being. The world — the nameable aspects of reality — is always subsequent to the Tao that cannot be named.

We may call this beginning the mother of the world. It is the moment, the period, the phase when the Tao takes form, and from such taking form the ten thousand things arise. What is motherly about this is the issuance of finite things from a great reservoir of possibilities. Like children issuing from the womb, the ten thousand things both do and do not express the potency of their source. Each is a definite something, and yet by being definite any one manifests only an aspect, a portion, of the overall maternal fecundity.

Another favorite Taoist figure is the uncarved block. A block is richer when uncarved than carved because it has more potential. Once it is carved it is fixed, limited. As long as it is uncarved, it can still be a chair, or a toy, or a statue. The Tao itself, considered in its aboriginal hiddenness, is more potential than actual. Even the ten thousand things of creation represent a specification that limits the unbounded capacity of the pre-creative Tao. So the mother mediates between the unlimited Tao and the various participations in the Tao's potential. The mother is a way-station, a bridge.

Having explored this maternal dimension of the world, the wise person goes on to learn about what the mother brings forth — the character of the world that the manifest Tao brings about. For Lao Tzu, the way to know the things of the world is to know their origin. The basic character of anything in existence derives from its source, the Tao that is the sole font of existence. Nothing that one can learn about particulars, including individual human beings, is so significant as the character of the sole font. Everything significant about a creature derives from its origins in the mysteriousness of the Tao. Without this mysteriousness, a thing is just a thing — flat, two-dimensional. A thing becomes interesting when the mysteriousness of its origins makes it swell into three dimensions. Then it has depth, as well as height and extension. Then it can be symbolic as well as literal. The more vital, feisty the human spirit, the more symbolic the world it perceives and loves to dwell within. The Taoists were extremely vital, feisty spirits. Lao Tzu and Chuang Tzu are as fresh today as when they first began exerting an influence because they were absorbed with the paradoxes of existence. Only these paradoxes do not go out of style. Only thought that deals with the radical foundations of the human condition gives the human spirit nourishment in season and out.

In sending the human spirit, or the sage-to-be, back and forth from the mother to the child, and then back to the mother, the Lao Tzu prescribes the basic dialectic of philosophy. One has to

ask why there is something rather than nothing, and then wonder about the particular somethings that have emerged, but then
return to the mysterious source that explains how the divide between nothing and something gets crossed. Taoists who made
the Lao Tzu and Chuang Tzu their scriptures went in for yogic
exercises. Letting their spirits escape from literal interests, they
traveled to the frontiers of the imagination, or to the imageless
depths of the interior spirit, to deal with the primordial Tao directly. The reason they kept returning, time after time, was that
dealing with the primordial Tao directly brought a unique satisfaction. Only in the holism and darkness of the most ultimate
mystery did the ancient Taoists find full nourishment. I believe
that this remains true for us present-day Americans. Only when
we are moving out to deal with divine mystery directly, in an
exodus from the familiar and explained, do we enter upon the
promised land, where we find rest for our spirits and know our
true home.

When we hold fast to this mother, this progenitor of our spirits, we meet with no danger. We are secure in the lap of the most
original thing we can find, so we feel safe from the deficiencies
of all lesser beings. History and geography can never satisfy us.
Always they threaten to leave us chained to the partial, however
diverse. To fall into the partial, when we have an inkling of the
total, is to feel threatened terribly. The partial has about it the
horror of the unexplained and unsecured. We fear we may sink
into nothingness, or that our spirits may be eternally frustrated,
finding no adequate explanation. It is amusing, paradoxical, and
revealing all in one that the only adequate explanation is to learn
that we cannot learn. In the end, like Socrates, we are happiest
confessing that we do not know, that it is all too much for us,
too mysterious.

It seems to me that the difficulties present-day Americans have
with this perennial wisdom cut across sexual lines. It is not as men
or women that the radical mysteriousness of God threatens us but
as creatures. We are utterly equal in our creaturehood, equally
condemned to find our fulfillment in a cloud of unknowing. The
Taoist sage speaks for men and women alike when describing how
contemplation of ultimate mystery makes him idiosyncratic: "My

mind is that of a fool — how blank! Vulgar people are clear. I alone am drowsy. Vulgar people are alert. I alone am muddled" (20/47). There is a clarity that is a sign of superficiality and a blankness that bespeaks awareness of the profound mysteriousness of everything in the world. There is a muddledness that comes from meeting God, and an alertness that bespeaks a forgetfulness of God. If we want to find anything like the full import of Taoism for feminists, we have to contemplate a text like the Lao Tzu deeply enough to let it strip us of our bearings. Only when we have let ourselves drift out to sea, away from the familiar and charted, will we touch the forces of significant orientation and creativity. We need a shift of mind that is a seachange. That is the implication of any serious call for conversion, religious or feminist. We need to know from having gone into our own depths or explored outside our prior harbors how profoundly equal women and men are in their need for God. When this conversion occurs, lesser issues (such as how to institutionalize equality) seem almost indifferent. How a given people renders the sexes equal means much less than that they do. That they do is an imperative bursting out of the depths of the contemplative experience that all human beings are held by the Tao. How they do is very important in coloring a given culture, but ultimately any fair coloring is acceptable. Men may control the overt power and women the covert. Men may command and women persuade. The apparent freedom of one may be the obverse of the actual freedom of the other. (For example, men's option to hold office may release women for more important creativity.) These arrangements matter less than holding fast to the mother and so finding the world to be rich beyond imagination.

~ ~ ~

Though beings oppressed by karmic woes endure innumerable sorrows, Kuan Yin's miraculous perception enables her to purge them all. No matter what black evils gather — what hell-spawned demons, savage beasts, what ills of birth, age, sickness, death, Kuan Yin will one by one destroy them. To the perfection

of her merits, to the compassion of her glance, to the infinitude
of her blessings, worshipping, we bow our heads.[4]

Kuan Yin is the most famous bodhisattva in East Asia. A feminine
form of the Indian Avalokiteshvara, she functions as a goddess of
mercy. Her special province is the needs of women in childbirth
and home life, but she is open to petitioners of both sexes and
all ages. From her face shines a motherly understanding and care.
Her iconography assures Buddhist believers that they have a safe
harbor, a sure recourse against all storms. We might say that in
her the eternal feminine has an especially gracious and kindly
countenance. She is the mother that all children project, the warm
and safe source from which we all issued and to which we all
long to return.

When we reflect on the specific assertions of this text, we enter the realm of popular Chinese Buddhist faith. Buddhism came
to China early in the Common Era. It intermingled with native
shamanistic, Confucian, and Taoist themes, and traditional Chinese culture never required people to discard one tradition while
using another. So the same person could pray to Kuan Yin and
practice a Confucian political science. It would not have been impossible to petition Kuan Yin and muse about the motherly Tao
contemplated in the Tao Te Ching. Sophisticated Chinese might
have been able to reduce their convictions to a few basic assertions
and account the rest symbolic, but the majority crossed vocabu-
laries constantly, speaking now of (shamanistic) divination, and
then of Buddhist karma, and a third time of Confucian virtue, and
a fourth time of Taoist "not-doing" (*wu-wei* — the passive action
characteristic of the Tao and the female). Here the language is
Buddhist.

Karmic woes are the fate of all people not yet liberated into nirvana. Thus they are another name for the pains and trials that no
one escapes. The Buddha's basic precept, "All life is suffering,"
echoes in these lines. To be human is to know sorrow, disappointment, pain, and finally death. Kuan Yin knows all about the
karmic condition of her followers. Like the Buddha during his
night of enlightenment, she can perceive just where each person
stands on the road to liberation. With this knowledge, she can

purify people of their faults, release them from their binds. She has the wisdom that has gone beyond karmic existence. She sees from the far side of the earthly, imperfect human condition and so knows exactly what each petitioner needs.

Apart from the particulars of Buddhist theology, one can see that the power attributed to Kuan Yin gives believers reason to write a blank check of faith. If the goddess knows everything and is all powerful, then no human turmoil or bind need be ultimate. For any problem, Kuan Yin is a sure recourse. This means that no problem need bring the believer to despair. No matter what happens, there is always a positive force greater than the negativity the believer may suffer or contemplate. That is why one can call Kuan Yin a goddess (a female face for divinity) in all accuracy. She is functioning with the total capacity that "divinity" implies. All things in human experience come under her sway and can be changed by her power.

The second stanza enumerates some of the evils that human beings have to fear. Be they spiritual (demons), physical (beasts, probably more symbolic than actual), or the negative realities of the life cycle, Kuan Yin is more than equal to the task of subduing them. The effect of the second stanza of our text is simply to amplify or reenforce the first. Many Buddhist texts employ a logic of reiteration. By saying the same thing several different ways, the message comes through that *nothing* is excluded. By implication, all the other scenarios that one could imagine are covered. The goddess is powerful always and everywhere. Just as the Buddha is "skillful in means to save," so that he can help every sinner or downtrodden person, no matter what his or her circumstances, so Kuan Yin has all situations under control.

The final stanza of our text moves from petition to praise. Petition is a worthy form of religion, but praise is purer, because the quotient of self-interest is smaller. So here the devotee of Kuan Yin praises the perfection of her merits. She has such a history of good deeds that she has gained the pinnacle of Enlightenment. The compassion of her glance shows her to be a Buddhist saint of the highest order. Compassion is the signal Buddhist virtue. Those who know most are most forgiving. Kuan Yin is moved by her knowledge of all creatures' karmic conditions to intercede on their behalf. An unconditional acceptance radiates from her face. These are her beloved children, and she is more interested in wiping away their tears than in exacting justice for their misdeeds. Those who know the history of devotion to her are aware that she has been a font of mercy for centuries. At the shrine to Kuan Yin in Tokyo (where she is called Kannon), one can see pictures of babies that delighted parents have attributed to her intercession. Each shrine to the goddess is a reminder of how many people believe in her, how many people have had their prayers answered. Bowing low, the devoted follower places everything in her keeping. This is true worship: attributing to a holy figure the power of the creator and redeemer — the power to make the world right and quiet the human spirit in peace and joy.

East Asian women were the special devotees of Kuan Yin, but many men also approached her. On the whole, East Asian cultures have thought of divinity in feminine terms, because in their families the mother has been the main source of emotional warmth. Fathers have tended to distance themselves from children, for a variety of reasons. Mothers have had a special need to bind children to themselves as a source of power in domestic politics. So when it came to imagining how the compassion of the Buddha would function, millions of Chinese, Japanese, and other East Asians gravitated toward Kuan Yin. She was, in effect if not doctrine, the most popular expression of the gracious power of Enlightenment to save people from their woes.

Many present-day feminists want to avoid stereotypes, under the sensible conviction that women have had opportunities closed to them because of popular notions of what was or was not feminine. Relatedly, feminists have wanted to honor the great range of intellectual and emotional characteristics that cut across divisions between the sexes: the rationality of women, the emotion of men, the logic of sensitivity (*esprit de finesse*) that both can possess. Granted this, however, I would like to continue to associate with the feminine aspects of divinity such as those manifested by Kuan Yin, in part because this still is sufficiently novel in the West to make it a way of challenging our assumptions about God. The more we can let divinity be the utterly creative love that we know abstractly it has to be, the better our religion is likely to become.

We know the Isaian figure of a nursing mother. God can no more abandon Israel than a nursing mother can abandon her child. We are less familiar with Kuan Yin, but she says much the same in another vocabulary: there is nothing threatening in human experience that divinity does not reckon and have both the power and the will to change on human beings' behalf. Both figures elicit the carte blanche of deepest faith. Both go below the level of argument, circumvent the problem of evil, and represent the complete answer that our hearts require: nothing can separate us from the love of God. Perhaps feminists who cannot accept such a religious possibility when they hear it couched in Western terms will reconsider it when it comes in the person of Kuan Yin. Perhaps the very audacity of the claim will bring home its revolutionary potential. Because we all exit into mystery, we all need grounds for hope. Kuan Yin has served millions of East Asians as a great ground for hope, so whatever she can do for us Americans will put us in good company.

~ ~ ~

Morning: read prayers with mother and sister-in-law for two hours. Since brother's death sister-in-law has been fasting, reading prayers, and constantly talking with me about the Buddhist life. When the great sorrow came to her, she almost wanted to give up living; now she seems determined to follow Buddha's way.[5]

This text comes from the diary of a Chinese woman published in 1927. The larger context is that two young women, sisters-in-law, encourage one another to enter a Buddhist nunnery. The one featured here has lost her husband after only three years of marriage. The writer, the husband's sister, is stimulated by the widow's example and eventually follows her into the convent. The widow has little difficulty gaining the permission of her in-laws (whose family she had joined at marriage). The sister of the dead man faces great opposition. In fact, her parents arrange to betroth her to a young man. This causes a crisis in her life and she arranges to enter the nunnery secretly, presenting her parents with a *fait accompli*. They are quite upset, but they allow her to remain in the convent. So the two sisters-in-law both become nuns, responding to the longing that the death in their family has stirred in their hearts.

People familiar with stories of Christian nuns will note striking similarities. The appeal of the monastic life can be both negative and positive. On the one hand, sorrow can make people dissatisfied with life in the world. Monastic life, in which one has renounced worldly attachments, can seem like a protection against such pains as the loss of a spouse. On the other hand, few religious vocations endure unless there is also a positive appeal. The life of silence, simplicity, prayer, and sharing ideals with others can seem much more substantial than life in the world. The work, pursuit of pleasure, family responsibilities, and other matters that preoccupy the majority of people can seem insubstantial. The more one has been shocked by death, or drawn to contemplate the mysteriousness of divinity, the more attractive a life focused on ultimate things can seem.

Chinese culture stressed family responsibilities so strongly that it was bound to feel ambivalent about the monastic life. To assume vows of celibacy and remove oneself from one's clan ran counter to Confucian standards. But in the measure that Buddhism gained respect in Chinese culture parents faced pressures to let their children follow a religious calling. As in Christianity, Buddhist monasticism argued that nothing was more imperative than following the call to save one's soul. If a person, male or female, felt a strong desire to live the monastic life, parental and familial concerns ought to fall away. Parents could be mollified by the argument that what the son or daughter was doing would benefit all the members of the family, improving their karma. Whatever any family member did to assist the vocation of a monk or nun would help that person draw closer to Enlightenment. Moreover, the monk or nun would be praying for the well-being of the family and benefiting the dead. Buddhism came to dominate funerary rites in East Asia because its doctrine of karma, along with its impressive ceremonies of chantings and bowings, of bells and incense, made it seem the most profound response to death.

The argument for monastic life could also be put in terms of the paradoxes of "life" and "death." Though the Chinese laid great stress on progeny, to continue the life of the clan, they realized that all physical life is subject to decay. The Buddhist argument that only by solving the problem of suffering could one gain true freedom struck many Chinese forcibly. Whereas old age was the great goal, even old age would end. If one could defeat the threats death raised against human meaning by moving one's spirit to a place where death could not touch it, one would have accomplished a greater success than anything one could accomplish physically. The serenity of the Buddhist nun or monk therefore became a powerful symbol in Chinese culture. Even though they didn't like it, the parents of the two women mentioned in this text had to bow to the superiority of the religious vocation the women were beginning.

The religious vocation continues to appeal to some women, often for feminist reasons. Joining a group of women dedicated to prayer and social service can seem a way of entering upon a more substantial life than what one might find in secular work or marriage. Also, women who fear that ordinary work and domestic life would subject them to patriarchal patterns can hope that joining a community of religious women will advance their liberation. Even when the group comes under the jurisdiction of male church leaders, the women can arrange that, on a day-by-day basis, they largely determine their own affairs. When such a feminist goal motivates religious women, one finds an interesting subversion of the patriarchal claims of both secular and religious authorities. The obedience that the women offer is less to the men officially in charge of the parent religious body than to their own instinct that they have the right to search for God according to their own lights.

Is there anything more basic than the right to search for God according to one's own lights? Most traditional cultures, such as the Chinese, have not emphasized individual liberties or the priority of individual conscience. Rather, they have emphasized people's responsibilities to their families, or the general cultural mores, or the common good. Women have been more subject to these controls than men, because so many traditional cultures have placed women in the keeping of their fathers, husbands, or elder sons. So an option for monastic life, when it expressed an individual woman's desire to make divine mystery, rather than anything male or familial or secular, the center of her life, was quite radical. It said that God is the only one who can rightly command a person's conscience. It said that when the chips are down and the bottom line is clear, only the divine mystery has the status of a truly sovereign power.

Many religions have taught that true freedom comes from surrendering to the will of God, or the Buddha, or the Tao. Many artists and scientists have followed their vocations with a religious passion, because they have felt that only responding to the appeal that painting or research made deep in their souls would bring them contentment. There are analogies in personal relations: responding to a love because one feels that it carries the seeds of one's destiny. In all these cases, when the force that one is obeying seems uniquely significant (to the point of being sacred), people can realize that their selves are bound up with their calling. They can realize that they cannot be who they feel they want or have to be if they do otherwise.

It is a sign of women's progress toward the full realization of their equal humanity that their freedom to pursue their vocations has expanded dramatically in recent decades. Even though fewer women are entering upon monastic vocations, many more women are entering upon careers that have vocational potential. The religious among us need to help such women clarify what makes an attraction truly significant. Only when the pathway seems likely to engage the person with the mysteriousness of the human condition and make that mysteriousness beautiful can we be confident that the attraction is a significant calling. Only when such matters as death and creativity, healing and social service, come to the fore, should we rejoice. Clearly these things did come to the fore for the two women in our text, so we should celebrate their liberation as a feminist victory. By handing themselves over to the Buddha, the Dharma, and the Sangha, they were taking control of their own destinies. By losing their lives, they were gaining them.

5

Japanese Texts

When they go on voyages across the sea to visit China, they always select a man who does not comb his hair, does not rid himself of fleas, lets his clothing get as dirty as it will, does not eat meat, and does not lie with women. This man behaves like a mourner and is known as the "mourning keeper." When the voyage meets with good fortune, they all lavish on him slaves and other valuables. In case there is disease or mishap, they kill him, saying that he was not scrupulous in observing the taboos.[1]

This text is from one of the earliest accounts of the Japanese people, a Chinese observation written before 300 C.E. The earliest native Japanese texts come over four hundred years later. The culture that this vivid description brings before us was deeply caught in a mentality of taboos. The journey across the sea to China was dangerous, and to deal with danger the ancient Japanese tried to placate the forces they felt could harm them. The man selected to be the potential scapegoat has to violate ordinary rules of hygiene. He must exist in a special status, changing his being so as to symbolize the special time the people are undergoing. He wants to be as unattractive to the ghostly forces as possible. He is already jousting with death, and by his peculiar uncleanliness he becomes someone that the forces of misfortune should not want to strike down. By playing this role, he allows his people to externalize their fears. The combination of dirt and cleanliness in his behavior marks him off as someone not easily classified. By not eating meat or dealing with women, he gains the power of

111

the ascetic. By not washing he shows himself indifferent to how he feels — another form of asceticism.

Ancient Japanese culture seems to have been shamanic. It was much concerned with taboos, ways of placating potentially destructive spirits, ways of getting forces of good spiritual influence on its side. When Buddhism became influential in Japan (after the sixth century C.E.), the native traditions, which had been customary rather than articulated or codified, had to become more explicit. "Shinto" is the name for these native traditions as rendered explicit. "Shinto" means the Way of the Kami, and it offers a deliberate parallel to Buddhism as the Way of Gautama (or the Middle Way, or the Way to Enlightenment).

The kami are the multitude of holy forces that the Japanese have always found in nature. Powerful human beings could be considered kami, but the majority of the eight hundred thousand gods of Shinto have been energies of nature. Anything strikingly beautiful or powerful or significant could be considered a kami. Physical shapes reminiscent of male and female organs, storms, lovely pools, rainbows — virtually anything of moment could qualify. Ancient Japanese religion is a good example of the thesis one finds among historians of early religions: the holy can attach itself to any object. If seen in the right light, any rock or animal or natural phenomenon or human functionary can manifest the sacredness of being. Such sacredness is both appealing and repelling. It arouses both desire and fear. In considering how to deal with the special event of a sea voyage to China, the ancient Japanese instinctively produced a ritual to express their ambivalent feelings.

Feminine forces played a stronger role in the oldest system of taboos and myths than in later centuries, when Chinese ideas (Confucian, Taoist, Buddhist) strengthened Japanese patriarchalism. Originally women partook of the mysteriousness that most ancient peoples have found in sexual desire and fertility. The indication in our current text is that when the ancient Japanese wanted to purify themselves, they refrained from sexual relations. The conviction probably was that sexual relations weakened people's spiritual power, leaving them vulnerable to malign influences. In other contexts, the Japanese could carry out rituals designed to rouse the forces of fertility. Here the fear seems to be of death and failure, so sexual intercourse becomes distracting.

We know from other sources that blood taboos have been influential throughout Japanese history. To have contact with a corpse or dying person rendered one polluted. Similarly, to have contact with a menstruating woman, or a woman who had recently given birth, put one out of sorts with the kami. One had to be purified. Japanese religion has always spent considerable energy on rites of purification. Many of these have been quite physical: bathing, sprinkling salt, burning clothing worn when one came into contact with death or blood. At the leading Shinto shrine (Ise, which was founded at the very beginning of the Common Era), priests would make sure that the main buildings were torn down and rebuilt every twenty years. Shinto preferred natural to adorned wood, gardens that were little tended, streams full of vegetation rather than streams artificially cleansed. Several different kinds of purity helped the traditional Japanese to feel that they were in harmony with the kami. To be out of harmony with the kami was to court disaster, while to gain harmony with the kami was to position oneself for good fortune.

Ancient Japanese women found their lives shaped by these Shinto convictions. Women's greatest value was their fertility, but they had to be careful how they exercised it. Because of their association with blood, they could be a source of pollution. Because of the weakness that sexual intercourse could create, they had to segregate themselves from men on solemn occasions. Under the influence of Chinese cultural ideals, Japanese women became submissive, as Confucian thought wished them to be. In the Shinto substratum of Japanese culture, however, the feminine principle continued to be something coeval with the male.

Chinese folklore held that the *yin* of women was as basic an ingredient as the *yang* of men. Ancient Japanese culture felt the same way, making feminine symbolism as fitting for the kami as masculine. By the time that Japan had developed a strong code for warriors, the image of the ideal Japanese woman was that of a very strong personality. Perhaps harkening back to the early queens, the wives of noblemen and warriors were expected to match their husbands in discipline. The greatest concern of any nobleman concerning his wife was her chastity, so the typical woman of social significance was supposed to be willing to die rather than be compromised sexually. Just as a warrior (samurai) was supposed to offer to kill himself if he failed the lord he was serving, so the wife of a significant Japanese man would sacrifice anything to uphold her honor (which reflected on the honor of her husband or father).

The archaic taboos surrounding women, and the medieval concern for honor, remind us how much changed with the development of Western modernity. Relations between the sexes had been much more formal. In part that was because precisely personal (subjective) considerations were little developed. Even more, however, it was because both men and women felt themselves to be assigned cosmic roles. They fit into patterns considered encoded in the cosmos to keep human beings harmonious with the sacred life-force. The myths spelled out how the ancient kings and queens, or the first human beings who had arisen to become the parents of all the rest, had behaved. The instinct of the ancient Japanese was to imitate this behavior. Thus even ordinary social interactions had something archetypal about them. Even ordinary social interactions were ritualized.

This tendency was probably strongest among the middle and upper classes, but it had its equivalents among the peasantry. Indeed, inasmuch as they lived closer to nature, the peasantry tended to assimilate the male and female forces to the powers that made the crops flourish and the animals plentiful. To be fertile in children and fields or animals was to receive the blessing of the kami and the life-force. This was the primary definition of good fortune. When Buddhism entered Japanese culture, it was adapted to meet this prevailing scheme. Leading bodhisattvas became kami, and kami became bodhisattvas. Throughout, women and men both sought to keep the taboos that would avoid ill-fortune or pollution, which now were considered functions of bad karma.

~   ~   ~

Now the male deity turning by the left, and the female deity by the right, they went round the pillar of the land separately. When they met together on one side, the female deity spoke first and said: "How delightful! I have met with a lovely youth." The male deity was displeased, and said: "I am a man, and by right should have spoken first."[2]

—Nihongi, I:11

This text comes from one of the two early editions of the ancient Shinto traditions. Prior to our verses, the primal couple have presided over the creation of the Japanese islands (which for Shinto was the beginning of the world). They are both Adam and Eve, the first human beings, and creative deities. Our verses are the prelude to their coupling to produce the human race. It is amusing, and instructive, that from the very beginnings of their relationship, as the traditional mythology depicts it, the male presses to predominate.

By the first decades of the eighth century C.E., when the chronicles were published, Chinese influence in Japan was considerable. It is difficult to know, therefore, whether the earliest strata of Japanese culture were as patriarchal as this text implies. After our verses, the male insists that they circumambulate the pillar again, and that this time he speak first. That should reverse the bad luck set in motion by the woman's having improperly taken the lead. The pillar is the connection between heaven and earth. In processing around it, the couple are in effect ritualizing their relationship with the blessing of heaven. They want to establish on earth the patterns that heaven will bless. For early Shinto, things on earth would ideally imitate things in heaven.

The first woman seems compliant enough. She is willing to redo the ceremony (anything to keep peace?). Her error was to be too enthusiastic. She liked the looks of the man and expressed her feelings. He is presented as more solemn. What they were up to, in ritualizing the production of the race, was a grave business. Among the many sanctioned ways for men and women to interact in traditional Japanese culture, one was for men to carry the burdens of authority and women to provide relaxation and relief. The geisha has institutionalized this pattern. For centuries she has allowed Japanese men to cast aside the burdens of responsibility and distract themselves with beauty, music, gay conversation, and (sometimes) sex. For the primal woman to appear as the lighter of the two sexes, or even as the slightly comic bungler, casts an intriguing light on Japanese sexual relations.

As the story unfolds, the couple next discover their sexual differences, which they find appealing. The surplus of the man seems to fit the lack of the woman, and they experience that together they make a fine fit. From their intercourse come more islands, so the symbolism is that creation is the result of sexual relations among the gods. The Japanese islands, it follows, are divine. They have a special relation to the primal couple, and one might consider them the central spot from which creation expanded. Such an ethnocentric view of creation is not unique to Japan (many people have thought that they and their land were the navel of the body of creation), but it played a significant role during the Shinto nationalism of the twentieth century.

From the account of the interaction of the first couple, one might draw two conclusions about relations between men and women. First, the two are coordinated to one another in mutual attraction and mutual need. Second, the male is to take the lead, because that is how their natures have deemed that they should interact. The coordination in mutual attraction and mutual need saves the story from any oppressive patriarchalism. From the beginning, humanity was both dual and unified. When Western egalitarians meet traditional patriarchal cultures, they can miss such cultures' ways of honoring the equal necessity of the female and male. For most truly ancient cultures, heterosexuality was so objective a feature of nature that it was simply assumed in all cultural reflection. Women might have less overt status or power than men, but the culture as a whole was so preoccupied with fertility that the necessity and so the value of women was obvious.

Moreover, it is not clear from our verses how oppressive the self-assertion of the male was thought to be. Clearly, throughout Japanese history men have had such a preponderance of power that women were always at risk. Men could abuse their power, and male power always circumscribed women's roles. But in this text the woman deflects the man's irritation with an easy compliance. She seems agreeable to whatever he feels is necessary for ritual propriety. One implication may be that she herself takes ritual propriety lightly. It does not matter to her who speaks first and who speaks second. What matters is that they speak agreeably, so as to forward their interaction and produce a good result. She is more interested in the relationship than its rules. Those who have followed the debates about Carol Gilligan's views of ethical differences between girls and boys will find something quite familiar. In Gilligan's view, girls are regularly more interested in preserving and nourishing relationships than in creating or obeying abstract rules. It would be stretching any interpretation of this text from the Shinto chronicles to find a Japanese equivalent of Gilligan's characterization, yet if one were forced to describe the couple in Gilligan's terms, the Japanese woman would fit the pattern more than not.

When Freud asked what women want, he spoke from some bewilderment. Cross-culturally, the interactions between the sexes produce bewilderment on both sides. For the pleasure in it, I have imagined the inner reflection of the primal Japanese woman, as she interacted with the primal Japanese man. She doesn't understand why speaking first is so important to him. She had no thought of following, or not following, a ritual pattern. They were walking around the pillar, getting themselves in the mood to establish on earth something worthy of heaven. They were enjoying the freshness of creation, when nothing had yet been spoiled. In her freedom and joy, she let the delight of her eyes direct her tongue. She would not say that his correction of her amounted to a fall from grace, an introduction of second-guessing, but it did cast a slight shadow. Wanting to get rid of this shadow and restore the sunny sense that everything could be made beautiful on earth, she smiled sweetly and fell in with his desire to redo the ritual circumambulation. When she found that this compliance pleased him (he drew himself up, he expanded his chest), she made a mental note. If it was as easy as this to restore good feeling between them, the future should not be too demanding.

How important was good feeling between them? More important than he seemed to realize. After all, there were only the two of them. No other ways of being human were in sight. If they did not get along well, this whole new venture of starting a lineage would be a nasty business. And if she understood the implications of their physical differences, they were going to have to manage some intimate coordinations. As the smaller and more vulnerable, she would have to be sure that he did not act brutally. So, why not move him away from anger and competition? Why not put their interaction on a new footing, one where they would cooperate, complement one another, rather than clash? True, at some point she might have to remind him that who spoke first was really quite arbitrary, just as she might have to remind him that her role in bringing forth their offspring was more prominent than his. Realism would demand acknowledging these facts in some way. But the way could be hers, and not his. The way could be implicit, a thing of emotion, as easily as a thing of laws. Laws were blunt instruments, good enough in their own way but much less interesting than smiles and intuitions. Why settle for the blunt, the legal, when one could create something more playful and intriguing? Why make this dusty walk around the pillar into a forced march, when it could be something light and rhythmic — a dance?

~ ~ ~

The resplendent luster of this child shone throughout all six quarters. Therefore the two deities rejoiced, saying, "We have had many children, but none of them have been equal to this wondrous infant. She ought not to be kept long in this land, but we ought of our own accord to send her at once to Heaven, and entrust her to the affairs of Heaven." At this time Heaven and Earth were still not far separated, and therefore they sent her up to Heaven by the ladder of Heaven. They next produced the Moon-god. ... His radiance was next to that of the Sun in splendor. This God was to be the consort of the Sun-Goddess, and to share in her government. Therefore they sent him also to heaven.[3]

—Nihongi, I:19

This text from the early Shinto chronicles describes the establishment of the sun goddess, Amaterasu, and her consort the moon. The "deities" who beget these heavenly gods are the primal couple we have just seen walking around the cosmic pillar. (Their names are Izanagi and Izanami.) The sun is the most brilliant of their children, and so they want both to honor her and to establish her in heaven, where her divine status may be clearer and all may benefit from her radiance. The moon is the next best of their offspring and seems a fitting companion for the sun. In the primal time of this account, communication between earth and heaven is easy, so the sun and the moon soon shine in heaven.

Several consequences of this story bear noting. First, Amaterasu became the leading divinity of the Shinto pantheon and the ancestress of the royal family. The insignia kept at Ise to symbolize the authority of the royal family linked them with Amaterasu. Second, the text thinks of heaven as the privileged realm, yet it has the creator-deities functioning on earth. Obviously, then, the original Shinto mythology of creation mixed the relations between heaven and earth. Heaven had more prestige, but originally earth was close to heaven and partook fully of the creative power we now locate in heaven. Third, it is distinctive, if not unique, that the Japanese consider the sun feminine and the moon masculine. Usually the sun is masculine and the moon feminine. With the sky, the sun is usually polarized to the earth. The rains, warmth, and light of the sky fertilize the earth the way male sexuality comes upon female sexuality. The moon seems to play a role in the cyclicism of women's fertility, and patriarchal cultures likened the reflected character of the moon's light (pale and changing) to women's reflection of the primal humanity blazing forth in men. Precisely why the Japanese feminized the sun is not clear. The suggestion in this text is that female human nature had something blazing, lustrous, in it that male did not.

For the Japanese imperial line to have the sun goddess as its original ancestor helped to divinize the emperors and queens. On occasion women ruled in ancient Japan, either because there were no male heirs or as regents for an heir under age. However, the more usual arrangement was for kings to rule, and this meant that the force representing divinity on earth (the ruler as personified link between heaven and earth) was of a different sex than the ancestral divinity in heaven.

Perhaps the reason for this crossed relationship between the sun goddess and the earthly king was the East Asian desire for a motherly countenance in heaven (mentioned previously). Perhaps from as early as the dawn of Japanese memory the popular instinct had been that the maternal was a more desirable divinity than the paternal. Amaterasu was more a queen than a mother, but simply by being feminine she carried the potential for a motherly benignity.

Another possibility is that the Japanese thought of the sun as the force they most wanted on their side. To make the sun feminine would then have been an instinctive effort to assure that it shone warmly on the king, and through the king on the land and whole people. Any culture dependent on agriculture feels at the mercy of the key elements: sun, rain, wind. In Japan rain and wind are certain. The more problematic force is the sun. Could it be that the feminization of the sun was a way to bring this more problematic force to human beings' aid? Or was the feminization of the sun itself a reflection of a Japanese judgment that female nature was more motile and less dependable than male? These are not the sorts of questions that early mythologies can answer. Their value lies more in their power to make us wonder about stereotypes, ancient and recent.

As the rest of the Shinto mythology presents her, Amaterasu is not volatile or inconstant. We shall see that in her contests with the wind god, Susanoo, she is the long-suffering female and he the obstreperous male (or trickster). Moreover, a calm attends her residence at the Shinto shrines and her presidency over the royal lineage. Thus, the overall impact of her "personality" suggests a desire to think of the sun as a steady, maternal benevolence. That may have been more wishful thinking than mythopoetic description of how nature actually worked, but it had the effect of making Amaterasu an unambiguous force for good. Little of the power of the sun to scorch and wither comes through in the stories about her. Much more significant is her capacity to enlighten and warm.

Suppose, then, that early Japanese culture wanted to think

about women as sources of light and warmth rather than threatening sources of withering. This is not a suggestion that leaps off the page. The data are not so unambiguous that one is forced to find a will to make the feminine benevolent. But it does fit the majority of the data. What is interesting about it?

First, one can ask whether it is an effort to represent how feminine nature appeared to the majority of ancient Japanese or an effort to influence females to become benevolent. Perhaps both intents were at work, but I find the first more likely. Traditional Japanese women naturally have varied considerably and cannot be fit into any hard and fast characterizations. Yet on the whole they seem less shrewish than the women one meets in traditional Chinese literature. If our hypothesis about this shrewishness is correct (that it served as a safety-valve, necessary because of the oppressiveness of Confucian patriarchalism), its relative absence in traditional Japanese culture suggests that Japanese patriarchalism was not so oppressive as Chinese. Certainly, Japan took from China a Confucian ethics and social philosophy. However, something in the ancient Japanese veneration of female fertility, or in the tradition of healing developed by their female shamans, kept the Japanese from devaluing female humanity to the extent that the Chinese did.

This is all quite hypothetical, but it is one way of making sense of what some commentators have called the balance between the sword and the chrysanthemum. The sword clearly is the stereotypically male interest in aggression and force. The chrysanthemum is the aesthetic ideal expressed in floral arrangement, the tea ceremony, and refinement of manners generally. Though stereotypically feminine, such refinement played a strong role in many men's lives, just as discipline (if not aggression) played a strong role in many women's lives. One of the reasons that the feminist movement has had difficulty gaining a foothold in Japan has been the disinclination of Japanese women to compete for power and status on male terms (for example, in business and politics).

Some commentators offer the opinion that the traditional Japanese wife and mother has had sufficient power to satisfy her needs. (She usually controls the money, doling out an allowance to her husband, and she has nearly complete say in the upbringing of the children.) At any rate, we see in the prominence of the sun goddess an ancient Japanese intuition that heaven, the realm of ultimate power and the source of models for earthly life, far from being a purely masculine realm, has a feminine light and warmth as its leading feature. Perhaps the arrangement of the traditional Japanese family (as well as the lineage of the royal family) paid homage to this light and warmth, thinking it the best hope for the family's flourishing.

~ ~ ~

Amaterasu had made august rice fields of Heavenly narrow rice fields and Heavenly long rice fields. Then Susanoo, when the seed was sown in spring, broke down the divisions between the plots of rice, and in autumn let loose the Heavenly piebald colts, and made them lie down in the middle of the rice fields. Again, when he saw that Amaterasu was about to celebrate the feast of first-fruits, he secretly voided excrement in the New Palace. Moreover, when he saw that Amaterasu was in her sacred weaving hall, engaged in weaving garments of the Gods, he flayed a piebald colt of Heaven, and breaking a hole in the roof-tiles of the hall, flung it in. Then Amaterasu started with alarm, and wounded herself with the shuttle. Indignant of this, she straightway entered the Rock-cave of Heaven, and having fastened the Rock-door, dwelt there in seclusion. Therefore constant darkness prevailed on all sides, and the alternation of night and day was unknown.[4]

—Nihongi, I:40–41

This text portrays the ancient enmity between the wind and the sun, or between the forces of chaos and the forces of order. Amaterasu is credited with having created agricultural order, and perhaps also weaving. Susanoo is the personification of the part of human nature that resists ordering. Like the psychoanalytic id, he insists on breaking out impulsively. Many of his offenses are not only disruptive but also polluting. He profanes the holy rice field and new palace. (A piebald colt was not acceptable for sacrifice. Sacrificial animals were supposed to be pure in coloring.) When Amaterasu finally wounded herself on the shuttle, her patience broke. She determined to force the gods to choose between her and Susanoo. They would either have to live in darkness or bring the wind to heel. In later parts of the story, the gods beg her to come out and restore the light, so she wins. But the entire myth is full of rich overtones about the relations between the sun and the wind, order and chaos, light and darkness, and female and male.

The light of Amaterasu was both physical and spiritual. One cannot separate her benevolent influence on the crops (note the sacralization of cultivating rice) from the order that she bestows on the mind. The darkness that her withdrawal brings is as much spiritual as physical. Without the sun goddess, Japanese culture would wander in confusion, as though in the darkest night. The implications of this symbolism include the significance of the imperial family, descended from the sun goddess. Without their incarnation of her order, the nation would be in perilous darkness.

This account, and the more ancient one available in the Kojiki (the other ancient Shinto chronicle), represent the sun goddess as a refined *Hausfrau*. She lays out the rows of the royal rice fields, and she suffers the mischief or vandalism of the naughty boy Susanoo. She works diligently weaving clothes for the gods (her family), and her patience snaps when Susanoo pollutes her palace and hall. In the Kojiki, he excretes upon the royal throne. Not noticing this, Amaterasu sits down in his mess, and then draws herself up, sickened. His bathroom humor has gone too far. When he finally causes her to injure herself, she withdraws. Her reaction is not what one would expect of an Indian goddess such as Durga: wipe him out. It is the more complete rejection of the refined lady: have nothing to do with him, cast his crudeness outside the pale of social intercourse. But of course Amaterasu knows her own worth. Her withdrawal into the cave is a deliberate ploy to make the gods rally behind her. She will show them who is truly important and who is dispensable.

I am intrigued that so ancient a text should depict the sun goddess following feminine stereotypes. Part of the struggle between herself and Susanoo is what has gone on in schoolyards for centuries. Susanoo is taunting Amaterasu, to get her attention. "Look at me," he is saying. "See how naughty I can be." The neatness of Amaterasu, her precision and order, drive Susanoo crazy. He cannot behave that way, so he tries to discredit her behavior. She represents a civilizing influence that worries him. If he succumbs to it, he may lose much of his vitality. Certainly, he will lose much of his freedom. So he turns rogue, even criminal (sacrilegious). How far he expects to get is unclear. His offenses remain more obnoxious than truly destructive. He resembles nothing so much as a boy fighting against being civilized.

Japan came to think of itself as highly civilized, yet it always hoped to retain its vitality. Unlike China, whose refinement sometimes lost vitality, becoming overly feminized, Japan seldom lacked spokespersons for a military vigor. The warrior classes, who had considerable influence on Zen, kept alive the notion that spiritual discipline ought to bring one to an extreme alertness. The martial arts became a spiritual pathway. Certainly, this discipline opposes the self-indulgence of Susanoo, but it seems calculated to retain his energy. So Susanoo was not forgotten in later Japanese culture. Amaterasu never had it entirely her own way. She prevailed, in the sense that her light and warmth remained the great necessities, but a healthy tension with the forces of disorder and darkness remained. The Japanese psyche seemed to realize intuitively that a fully adequate culture is a conjunction of opposites. What may seem incompatible logically can become invigorating psychologically.

In a culture where the feminine can stand for both order and levity, in tension with a masculinity considered both impulsive and grave, one has the potential for a rich cross-fertilization between the sexes. Perhaps this is one of the most important sources of Japanese creativity. Commentators tend to underscore the Japanese genius for cooperative work, but this in itself involves many crossings of stereotypically male and female characteristics. So perhaps such cooperative work has been anticipated and prepared, psychologically, by myths such as those depicting the antagonism between Amaterasu and Susanoo. Perhaps in the depths of the Japanese psyche the sun and the wind forced people to remember that creativity demands a union of order and vigor on several levels.

If we translate these reflections for present-day American culture, one of the obvious lessons is the continuing need for men and women to interact. Included in this interaction are the stereotypes that each sex carries. Unless men are meeting with women's ways of ordering affairs, bringing discipline to nature and family life and expressing creativity, men will lack many useful counterbalances. Similarly, unless women are meeting with men's ways of ordering affairs, men's challenges to neatness and propriety, men's versions of how all people need to reach into the vulgar and offensive if they are not to become effete, women will lack many counterbalances they need.

In a time when women continue to long for a feminist spirituality and men are starting to seek a spirituality that takes their distinctiveness into account (if only in reaction to the women's movement), we should remind those of separatist inclination that some things become clear only when the sexes are together, interacting in ways that remind them both that the other's instincts have some validity. The physical differences between men and women (both endocrinological and anatomical), as well as the social differences, ensure that the sexes will always surprise one another. We may hope that such surprise is seldom as disagreeable as what Susanoo forced upon Amaterasu, but we are wise to prize our differences, as well as our similarities, and wonder at both.

~ ~ ~

The mouth of the Foundress is not different from that of an ordinary person, but the words spoken through the lips are those of God the Parent, and it is God the Parent Himself that is speaking through the mouth of the Foundress. Her outward appearance is quite similar to that of an ordinary person, but it is the mind of Tsuki-Hi, God the Parent that dwells in Her body. Therefore the teachings which were later given through the lips, through the pen, through action, and through wonderful salvation, are the very ones directly given by God the Parent.[5]

This text comes from an account of the origins of Tenri-kyo, one of Japan's most significant "new religions." Tenri-kyo arose following the possession of the woman who became known as the Foundress. She was first possessed by the force later known as God the Parent in 1838, and in 1908 her group was accredited by the government as an official Shinto sect. The woman, known after her possession as Miki Nakayama, is believed to be present in spirit at the central shrine of her group (in Tenri, Japan). Members of Tenri-kyo believe that Tenri is the center of the world, and that by the descent of a heavenly dew to the main pillar of the shrine a new age of peace and good will begins.

Miki was forty-one when God the Parent made her his mouthpiece. Her husband objected to the changes in their life that her new calling would necessitate, wanting her to remain a housewife. But as long as what she considered the will of God was being thwarted, Miki shook so severely that her family feared her great harm. Our verses express the theory of incarnation or possession on which Tenri-kyo depends. Miki served as the mouthpiece for a new revelation, in which the parenthood of God came to the fore and a messianic age was promised.

Commentators have often noted the continuity between an ancient shamanism that used women as the customary mouthpieces of the spirits and the new religions that developed during the nineteenth century (and spurted again after World War II). Traditionally, women went into trance to serve the bidding of spirits of the dead or spirits that could cure illnesses. Schools of such shamanesses developed, and they continued to be influential in rural Japan until World War II. Sometimes blind women were considered especially apt candidates. Older shamanesses taught novices techniques for going into trance, as well as herbal medicine and other staples of folk healing. Bands of shamanesses would travel regular routes throughout rural villages, offering counseling as well as physical healing. Their ministrations depended on the popular conviction that spirits and ghosts were real forces, and regularly they involved trance, divination, and rites of purification.

The sexual stereotype involved was that women were considered more susceptible to "takeover" by the spirits than men.

Extended, this rationale made the woman's familiar spirit her lover, with whom she could be involved in a lifelong affair. The most professional shamanesses did not marry, or were widowed, and many shrines (for example, the one at Mount Fuji) had shamanesses available for consultation. On religious holidays they could do a brisk business.[6] Historians of the Japanese folk arts sometimes suggest that puppetry and kabuki theater have roots in the healing practices of traditional bands of shamanesses.

The shamanic belief that women have more labile personalities than men, and so are more apt to be taken over by spirits, adds another interesting datum to our store of information about Japanese views of the sexes. Whether the story of Izanagi and Izanami walking around the pillar and working out the propriety of who should speak first had a direct influence on this perception is not clear, but it may have made an impact. The Western parallel would be the depiction of Eve in the Genesis account of the expulsion of the first human beings from paradise. The curiosity of Eve, and the suggestibility on which the serpent traded, were imputed to women as feminine characteristics. Perhaps something similar accrued to Japanese women from the account of the primal woman's having spoken first.

At any rate, it is instructive that many of the new religions have had female founders. The relationship between Miki and the divinity she served is more explicit than most on the matter of the foundress's fronting for the divinity, but it is not unique. In addition to the shamanic heritage, never too distant in Shinto, one might add that having a female founder has brought the maternal face of divinity close to new religionists. Both the nineteenth- and the twentieth-century circumstances that stimulated the rise of new groups were heavy with anxiety. Japan was being forced to end centuries of isolation from the West, and as a result its traditional cultural patterns were subject to reassessment. Neither traditional Shinto nor traditional Buddhism escaped criticism. Many doubts surfaced about the viability of both traditions, in face of the modernization represented by the West. Where would Japan find the strength to make the transition to a new self-understanding? The new religions tended to offer comforts based on age-old religious patterns. Grouping people in ways reminiscent of what went on traditionally in rural villages, they offered a strong sense of community to offset the threats of anomie that many found in the prospective changes. Relatedly, they offered a simple, demanding moral code that included the ideal of spending oneself for the good of the group — something that village culture also prized.

For Tenri-kyo, the divinity revealed through the foundress Miki was an appealing blend of the female and the male. As parental, this divinity bridged characteristics of both sexes. The accent, however, was on the care and intimacy that the divinity wanted to lavish upon followers. The moral code that Miki taught was simple, and its demands were more than offset by the message of encouragement that God the Parent offered. To people tempted to feel lost in the crowd, God the Parent was winningly personal and near. Much like Kannon (Kuan-Yin), God the Parent was a figure of mercy and help. Indeed, one of the first areas in which God the Parent specialized was the easy delivery of children — precisely the sort of help in which Kannon had specialized. The foundress Miki merely offered a new voice and message seeming to update the older sources of religious comfort.

Among the parallels that American religious history calls to mind, Mary Baker Eddy (1821–1910) certainly stands out. She had been sickly, and only by becoming the main spokesperson for Christian Science did she gain full vigor. Her message had a special appeal for women of the Victorian era suffering "the vapors" and other neurasthenic maladies. Eddy's Christianity was as original, or heterodox, as Miki's Shinto, and both put forward a message of positive thinking designed to convince people that divinity would guide them through the cultural changes surging around them.

Social analysts of religion sometimes make the argument that people on the margins of social power tend to be more open to revisionist interpretations than people at the centers of power. Establishments are slow to change, because the status quo is serving their interests very well. More times than not, women are the majority of those on the margins, if only because women are the majority of the poor ("the feminization of poverty" is the notion that women, and the children for whom women provide most of the care, make up the bulk of those on the welfare roles or living below the official indexes of poverty). So it is not surprising that women would be more open than men to interior voices urging a change from old religious ways and a new revelation. In the cases of Miki and Mary Baker Eddy, heeding the voices stirring within proved a path to healing. When others found the message relevant, the revelation became public — something for the cure of the many. Then the spokesperson felt that proclaiming the message, founding the new movement, and bearing the hardships entailed was providential. God willed this, and God could not be gainsaid. This was a more prophetic tone than what the ancient Japanese shamanesses tended to take, but like ancient shamanism the new religions (American as well as Japanese) have tended to trust private inspiration. In the case of female founders, the motif has been a marital bond with the inspiring divinity, making the foundress doubly the representative of the divinity. Because of her special intimacy with God the Parent, Miki led Tenri-kyo for the rest of her life, receiving the revelations that completed its stipulated doctrines and rituals.

~ ~ ~

In contrast to Americans, Japanese married couples do very little entertaining as a couple. Further, romance is not necessarily a concomitant of marriage, even as an ideal. Geisha are supposed to be sexy where wives are sober, artistic where wives are humdrum, and witty where wives are serious.... Certainly from an outside perspective, which by almost any lights shows Japan as an egregiously male-dominated society, this split nature of femininity seems unfair to women. Why can't wives go out with their husbands? Why can't geisha marry and work too? Why are there geisha at all? But Japanese wives and geisha themselves often have a different view of these institutions, one that we cannot simply dismiss as distorted or false consciousness.[7]

This description comes from a book on the geisha written by an American anthropologist who gained admittance to geisha circles. She had spent time in Japan as a child, spoke Japanese well, and lived for some months as an apprentice geisha, learning the life from the inside. Since the geisha are famous, or notorious, examples of the traditional Japanese attitude toward women, her study inevitably raised questions of justice, sexism, and female consciousness.

The split in femininity mentioned in the quotation is not absolute in Japan, but it has been strong. In other cultures a similar split has divided women into wives and mistresses. Geisha are not mistresses (although they can be). They are not prostitutes (although some get involved with patrons). On the whole, they are hostesses and entertainers. When a group of businessmen want to entertain clients or simply want to relax after a long day's work, they are likely to go to an establishment that offers food, drink, and geisha. The geisha serve the men as female companions. The more accomplished among them sing, or dance, or play a classical Japanese musical instrument. They dress beautifully, according to old Japanese aesthetic standards, and they are glamorous — lovely, witty, flirtatious. The men drop many inhibitions, even behave foolishly, and go home refreshed. Geisha are expensive, so frequently the tab goes on the firm's expense account.

The geisha vocation requires that women live apart from ordinary family life, in a ghetto of their own. Usually older geisha manage the establishments and train the younger geisha. If a woman wants to marry, she has to leave the geisha life. Enough geisha have illegitimate children to provide the geisha quarters with a family atmosphere of its own. Generally girls raised in the geisha life follow their mothers in the profession and fare quite well. Boys raised in the all-female atmosphere fare badly. Ironically, the geisha are one of the few groups of Japanese women who manage their own lives. The service they provide men has made them independent businesswomen and created a subculture in which men are quite secondary.

Why have so many cultures bifurcated femininity into domestic and romantic halves but not bifurcated masculinity in the same way? The geisha suggest that Japan has carried such a bifurcation to greater lengths than other countries, but one can find at least the seeds of such a division everywhere. Part of the reason seems to be the necessity of women's dealing with children and the likelihood of women's dealing with the practical tasks of a household. In traditional cultures men do not want to deal with either of these areas, whether because they have come to be considered women's work or because of the demands they carry. They are not glamorous, and only the love that women have for their children and husbands makes them bearable. How much this love is the product of biological evolution, developed as an energy necessary for survival, is hard to say. What seems clear, though, is that women's dependence on men for financial support has pressured them to accept the bifurcation of their image in most cultures. Women have had to marry and raise children, if they were to have a secure place in the social scheme of things. The women who avoided the domestic role, through work as geisha or prostitutes or other adornments of men's lives, have been at least as dependent on men as have wives and mothers. Only nuns have avoided a sexual tie to men, and both Buddhist and Christian nuns (the two main monasticisms) have had to deal with male-run institutions (the Sangha and Church).

Looking at Japanese women's acceptance of the geisha, one can marvel at the practicality of many women. Certainly, wives can be jealous of geisha, and geisha can be jealous of wives. But often the two groups of women seem to reach an accommodation, especially when the geisha are not sexual partners of the husbands but simply hostesses or entertainers. The wives focus on the children and household as their source of power and satisfaction. The wives also have a stake in their husbands' careers, advancing in status as their husbands advance in their firms. Publicly, a wife is honored in the measure that her husband is honored. So it is to her advantage to have her husband succeed, and this may explain wives' acceptance of the long hours the husbands work and the evenings they spend entertaining clients.

The geisha obviously have a stake in the bifurcated Japanese femininity. They have the glamor role, but it takes only a short while for them to realize how precarious their position is. They have none of the security or stability of the wife and mother. Most of the geisha have an artistic temperament and so find the lessons in dance, song, musical instruments, and the rest congenial. They join the subculture of artists and theater people, sharing the same teachers and often living in adjacent quarters. Some geisha also seem to enjoy the independence of men that life in their quarters affords. Inasmuch as they are content with their fate, they can thank the wives and mothers for making it possible. They could not do what they enjoy doing if they had to raise children and run a household.

The parallel for men might be a split between business and recreation. The typical Japanese executive marries to satisfy his family's interest in continuing their lineage. If not arranged by the family, his marriage certainly takes the family's interests into account and is a pragmatic venture. He might find romance, but he is more interested in gaining children and a well-run home. If he longs for an artistic life, he has to leave business circles. Business is too demanding to allow him a serious avocation. Indeed, business is too demanding to allow him an intense home life (spending large amounts of time with his children, for example). So his recreations are in the nature of escapes from the preoccupations of business or government work or his craft. After middle age he may use his home as a refuge, but until then he takes his vacations and recreations in patterns dominated by his firm, who are like an extended family.

One sees, then, how much both sexes have been constrained by the interests of society at large in their mating and other interactions. What individual men and women might work out on their own, were the pressures of their families or surrounding cultures not so great, demands considerable imagination. For several generations the West has been experimenting with this matter, but in historical perspective such experimenting is an aberration. As Japanese wives and geisha both know very well, the chances of "having it all" are slim, especially for women.

Conclusion
Eastern Lessons

We have reflected on texts from Islamic, Hindu, Buddhist, Chinese, and Japanese cultures. The texts have stimulated reminders about the assumptions of those cultures, the roles that women have played in them, and the religious outlooks that the cultures have used to estimate the place of women. Are there any clear lessons that this swath of world history and women's experience presents? Can we generalize about the experience of "Eastern" women, or have we only discrete cultural bits with little significance beyond their own narrow range of reference?

I am leery of grand generalizations regarding the sexes, because the more I learn about how women and men have interacted, the more complicated the overall patterns seem to be. There are women who bow to the conventions of their time and place, and women who flout them. Both groups have their counterparts in men. There are women who seem characteristically feminine in being practical — hardheaded as only mothers have to be. Yet there are also women who seem equally characteristically feminine in leaving heavy financial or political responsibilities to men and taking a lighthearted approach to life. Sometimes the same woman by turns is practical and lighthearted. Sometimes the same culture asks its women to be both more practical and more flighty than its men. After one has paid homage to the individual differences among women, and then to ethnic, religious, and historical differences, what remains? In this context, what remains for me is the validity of the observation that, on the whole, women are supposed to accommodate to men more than men are supposed to accommodate to women.

133

This runs in tandem with the observation that men assume that masculinity is the first instance of humanity and femininity the second. By this judgment men do not mean that women are not as populous or as necessary as men. They mean that when they think about "human nature" the characteristics that define it loom in their mind's eye as more masculine than feminine. Inasmuch as men have held the balance of cultural power in most societies, running the politics, economics, education, and religion, men have imposed this prejudice upon most cultures. Growing up in such cultures, women have shared the assumption that masculinity has an advantage when it comes to expressing the essence of being human. Certainly, women have also challenged this assumption, both unconsciously and consciously. Certainly, some men have known in their bones that the assumption was flawed and dangerous. But I believe that the texts we have explicated support the judgment that maleness has been the ordinary or normal mode of humanity and femaleness something extraordinary or abnormal — something not so reliable, regulative, or comprehensible.

For example, Muslim women are honored by the Qur'an, but not so fully as men. Hindu women are more dangerous than Hindu men. Buddhist women are a threat to the prosperity of the Sangha as Buddhist men are not. Chinese women were not fit pupils for Confucian sages. And Japanese women have not been the friends of Japanese men — the companions who could inspire such thoughts as the Greek "other half of my self." Were history written from the viewpoint of women in any of these cultures, one might receive a very different impression. But that is precisely the point: history has been written from the viewpoint of men in all these cultures, and that viewpoint has determined that women would be "other" and mysterious.

One might make the argument that biblical culture, classical Greek culture, and their Western offspring manifest the same pattern. The argument would be valid, but with a few qualifications. First, of the Eastern cultures that we have studied, only Islam presents a personal God who serves as the source of humanity (human beings are the images of this God) and so makes the ultimate judgment on their worth precisely personal. Compared to the biblical God, however, the God of the Qur'an limits the personal character of the relations between humanity and divinity. The God of the Qur'an is the Sovereign Lord, commanding absolutely (though compassionately and mercifully), while the biblical God makes covenants and incarnations that reduce the threat or distance latent in his sovereignty.

The Hindu gods and goddesses, the Buddhist images of the absolute, the Chinese Tao, and the Japanese kami all treat the human being as something less than a friend. They can be kindly, parental, even a lover, but they do not establish relationships that make friendship and equality between the sexes an obvious effect of the common status that men and women have as images of the divine. Qualifications to these bold assertions leap to mind as soon as one makes them (for example, Krishna is the servant and friend of Arjuna at the beginning of the Bhagavad-Gita; by the end, however, he is the awesome Lord of the universe). Moreover, the overtures of the biblical God toward equality and friendship are limited by his status as infinite Creator. So there is no iron-clad distinction between Eastern and Western outlooks on this point. Still, I think that there is a difference of emphasis. It seems to me that Eastern women have fewer precisely personal resources at the depths of their cultures from which they might draw forth images of their relationships with divinity and men to move them toward equality and friendship.

Whether or not this generalization is correct, I have found reflecting on Eastern texts a salutary reminder of how complicated and relational the images of women and men have been throughout history. Like the images of the divine, which cannot be separated from the images of ideal humanity to which they are correlative, the images of men and women run so close to the heart of any culture that they have to accommodate a great range of possibilities. There have to be images explaining female weakness and female strength, male weakness and male strength, the bedazzlement of women by men and of men by women, the antipathy of men to women and women to men.

Granted this, however, I find that women in most cultures have less antipathy toward men than men have toward women. One might say that women are more generous, or more in need

of establishing friendly ties, or less inclined to become antagonistic, or better able to live with confused signals. Whether by
upbringing or hormones, Eastern women, like Western women,
are more interested in the lives of men than their male counterparts are interested in the lives of women. Men are curious about
women, because they want to get women to do their bidding or
they want to avoid upsets to the status quo favoring men. But
men spend less time and energy musing about how women con-
figure the world or embody humanity than women spend musing
about the ways of men. The situation into which the majority of
men have been born has relieved them of the need to understand
women well. The situation into which most Eastern, and Western, women have been born has made understanding men (their
sovereigns, the ones holding their fate, the source of the children
the women have been so pressured to want) crucial for survival.

So women tend to understand men better than men understand women, and that has been a key to the survival of the
women we have seen reflected in these Eastern texts. They have
been very shrewd when it came to survival. They have known
with a connatural genius how to bend to the wind, soothe the potentially murderous ego, and make themselves desirable. Indeed,
they have tended to make themselves indispensable — as cooks,
tailors, sources of pleasure, sources of progeny, clerks, nurses,
and sometimes confidantes. What they have not created, by and
large, is traditional cultures that made female humanity the equal
of male humanity in both rights and duties. By and large, female
creativity has not become the equal of male, when the culture
went through its ordinary accounting procedures and distributed
its kudos. Some deeper thinkers might sit back and notice the female creativity shadowing virtually every male development, and
sometimes outshining many male developments, but the culture
at large tended to think of women's work as ancillary or derivative.

Theologically, the correlative was that nothing in their divinities forced the Eastern cultures we have considered to make
women's creativity as significant as men's. Women's creativity has
tended to be considered natural: making children. Men's creativity has dominated the cultural scene — the art, theology, science,

and politics. Inasmuch as culture was more prestigious than nature, the creativity of men overshadowed the creativity of women and rendered equality and friendship between the sexes problematic. The femininity of the Tao did not override this general state of affairs.

The Equality of Friendship

As I ruminate about the relations between the sexes that the world religions spotlight, my mind turns to the question of antidotes. So much has obviously been diseased, by today's egalitarian (feminist) standards, that one has to ask about cures. The cure that fascinates me now is the phenomenon of friendship. If we are to change the sexism that has ravaged relations between women and men in the past, if we are to rehabilitate marriage, parenthood, collegiality, church membership, and the other ways that the sexes struggle to share and develop their common humanity, we have to find a broad, affectionate, cooperative meeting of minds and hearts that will cut through past misperceptions and prejudices. Friendship is the force that might do the job, so let me conclude this book by reflecting on friendship between men and women, probing the hypothesis that it might deliver on the promise that the most encouraging of our Eastern texts have suggested.

Several years ago a friend was trying to explain to my husband and me the breakup of the marriage of a fourth person, whom he knew quite well and we knew slightly. This fourth person was charming, attractive, obviously of good will and manifestly in pain. He spoke of his children as the pleasure of his life, and so we wondered what had gone wrong with his marriage, to bring him to divorce and regret. The friend trying to explain the disaster, and so the man's guilt about the future fate of his beloved children, tried this analysis, and then that. But nothing worked until he finally said, "I told him that marriage was about friendship. He had not married a woman who could be his best friend. He had married a woman who turned his head, stirred his loins, and made him feel macho. Now he's paying a terrible price for his mistake."

Friends achieve an equality, a balancing of the scales, or they do not advance in their friendship. Regardless of how things look to outsiders, friends themselves know that each is contributing according to his or her resources and taking out according to his or her needs. Friendship is the most basic of communisms, and if the various followers of Karl Marx had taken this fact to heart we would not be speaking now about the death of communism in Eastern Europe. If leaders had thought of themselves as the friends of the people and "comrade" had not been diluted by cynicism, we might now be seeing in Eastern Europe and China wonderful demonstrations of evangelical brotherhood and sisterhood.

For friendship demands that two or more people find a way to interact as genuine equals. Unless they share mutual respect, mutual need, and mutual affection, their friendship withers on the vine. This is especially provocative when one recalls the Johannine Jesus telling his followers that he has not called them servants but friends. He has revealed to them all the things in his heart, and he invites them to reveal to him all the things in their hearts. This is a friendship with the divine that boggles any serious person. It is a fulfillment of the longing of the human heart for intimacy with God that startles one into realizing one had little idea how radically God wants to share existence with us human beings.

I believe that the future fortunes between the sexes depend on images of friendship gaining more weight than images of disjunction, let alone images of misogyny or misanthropy. We have to decide which experiences we are going to grant privileged status and which we are going to consider secondary or aberrational. As we ponder questions such as these, I believe that we do best by considering the friendship that arises in successful marriages. What has happened in the cases where women and men have built a life so common that in maturity they cannot think of self apart from spouse? How have they achieved such mutuality, and the fruitfulness it seemingly inevitably brings? One thing is clear: in successful relations between women and men, neither feels jobbed. Both know that they are more themselves together than either could have been apart. Each feels that the other is responsible for measures of the self that probably would have lain fallow, unrealized.

In the marriages that work, sexual attraction plays its part, but things of the mind and soul become more important. Two people realize that they understand one another as nobody else does. They realize that the other has become half of themselves, so that absence, whether real or imagined, is like the severing of a limb. Some of their bonding is intelligible, but much is mysterious — a matter of grace. How did it happen that they came to agree on so much? Even when they can point to painful battles, real work that each put out to advance their love, they know that what they have gained lies beyond their deserts. They have received far more than they have given. The blessing of their love, their friendship, has been out of all proportion to the price they have paid.

In the final analysis, the hope that women and men have to sustain is that they will both be able to say that God was wise to create humanity male and female. Too often the wisdom of the human condition has been questionable, especially for women. Too often women have had to wonder why it should be that, instead of being equal, femininity has been second class. Beyond power and opportunity, the worst inequality has been in affection. Again and again, women have felt that they gave much more affection than they received. They have felt that theirs were the tender hearts, and that this brought them the greater share of suffering. To redress this in the future, we shall have to overturn some of the most basic images bequeathed us by the religious traditions, Eastern even more than Western.

For example, we shall have to overturn the image of women as more natural than men and so less cultural. Even when this image offers boosts to women's status, as it may in cultures indebted to Taoism, it risks leaving women on the margins of human creativity: politics, education, science, religion. Relatedly, we shall have to define the personal as the crux of the divine revelations about the ways that humanity reposes in divinity and allow that male-female friendship, whether that of romance or that of collegiality, is the richest sort of personal challenge and support. Men can learn what it means to be fully human only when they have deep friendships with women, and women can learn about the full potential that humanity carries only when they have deep friendships with men.

Eastern women, subtle and creative despite the hindrances put in their way by patriarchal cultures, show us that one must never give up on relations between the sexes. These relations are too intimately tied to the origins of life, and too fascinating, for us to let disappointment make them suspect or fearful. So the Muslim women who, though wrapped and veiled, put bells on their toes to attract attention, live in my imagination as great witnesses to hope. No matter how oppressive their culture, they preferred to listen to the quickening of their hearts and believe that God, merciful and understanding, would not have put such a quickening there had it not been good. From that goodness, they could build scenarios of friendship and romance with men that might redeem the injustices caused by male, and female, suspicion. Those scenarios remain as poignant today, and as necessary, as they were a thousand years ago.

Notes

Chapter 1: Introduction: Religious Woman

1. For an overview of women's experiences with the world religions, see Denise Lardner Carmody, *Women & World Religions*, 2d ed. (Englewood Cliffs, N.J.: Prentice-Hall, 1989); Arvind Sharma, ed., *Women in World Religions* (Albany, N.Y.: State University of New York Press, 1987); Nancy Falk and Rita Gross, eds., *Unspoken Worlds*, 2d ed. (Belmont, Calif.: Wadsworth, 1989); Diana Eck and Devaki Jain, eds., *Speaking of Faith* (Philadelphia: New Society, 1987).

2. Denise Lardner Carmody, *Biblical Woman* (New York: Crossroad, 1988).

Chapter 2: Islamic Texts

1. All quotations from the Qur'an are from A. J. Arberry's *The Koran Interpreted* (New York: Macmillan, 1956).

2. Mary Morris, *The Waiting Room* (New York: Doubleday, 1989), p. xiii, quoting from Marguerite Duras's novel, *The War* (no data given).

3. See Jane I. Smith and Yvonne Haddad, "Women in the Afterlife: The Islamic View as Seen from the Qur'an and Tradition," *Journal of the American Academy of Religion* 47, no. 1 (Spring 1975): 39–50.

4. See Francine Prose, "Confident at 11, Confused at 16," *The New York Times Magazine*, January 7, 1990, 22 ff.

5. See Saadia Khawar Khan Chishti, "Female Spirituality in Islam," in *Islamic Spirituality: Foundations*, ed. Seyyed Hossein Nasr (New York: Crossroad, 1987), p. 205.

6. See Yvonne Yazbeck Haddad, "Islam, Women and Revolution in the Twentieth Century," in *Women, Religion and Social Change*, ed. Yvonne Yazbeck Haddad and Ellison Banks Findly (Albany: State University of New York Press, 1985), pp. 275–306.

7. See Jane Perlez, "Puberty Rite for Girls Is Bitter Issue across Africa," *New York Times*, January 15, 1990, p. 7.

8. For a treatment of Islam both comprehensive and consistently appreciative, see Isma'il R. al Faruqi and Lois Lamya' al Faruqi, *The Cultural Atlas of Islam* (New York: Macmillan, 1986).

Chapter 3: Hindu Texts

1. Raimundo Panikkar, *The Vedic Experience: Mantramanjari* (Berkeley: University of California Press, 1977), p. 82.

2. See William K. Mahony, "Upanishads," in *The Encyclopedia of Religion*, ed. Mircea Eliade (New York: Macmillan, 1987), 15:149.

3. Sarvepalli Radhakrishnan and Charles A. Moore, eds., *A Source Book in Indian Philosophy* (Princeton, N.J.: Princeton University Press, 1957), p. 83.

4. Raimundo Panikkar, *The Vedic Experience: Mantramanjari*, p. 123.

5. See R. N. Dandekar, "Vedas," in *The Encyclopedia of Religion*, 15:215.

6. David Kinsley, *The Goddesses' Mirror* (Albany: State University of New York Press, 1989), pp. 3, 267.

7. See, for example, Bernie S. Siegel, *Love, Medicine & Miracles* (New York: Harper & Row, 1988).

8. Kees Bolle, *The Bhagavadgita: A New Translation* (Berkeley: University of California Press, 1979), p. 13.

9. Radhakrishnan and Moore, eds., *A Source Book in Indian Philosophy*, pp. 189, 191.

Chapter 4: Buddhist Texts

1. Edward Conze, I. B. Horner, David Snellgrove, and Arthur Waley, *Buddhist Texts through the Ages* (New York: Harper Torchbooks, 1964), pp. 26–27.

2. Henry Clarke Warren, *Buddhism in Translations* (New York: Atheneum, 1973), p. 447.

3. Ibid., pp. 297–98.

4. Conze et al., *Buddhist Texts through the Ages*, p. 253.

5. T. W. Rhys Davids, *Buddhist Suttas* (New York: Dover, 1969), pp. 256–57.

6. Ibid., p. 257.

Chapter 5: Chinese Texts

1. D.C. Lau, *Confucius: The Analects* (New York: Penguin, 1979), p. 134.
2. James Legge, trans., *Book of Rites* (New York: University Books, 1967), 2:428. I owe this reference to Theresa Kelleher, "Confucianism," in *Women in World Religions*, ed. Arvind Sharma (Albany: State University of New York Press, 1987), pp. 141, 275.
3. D.C. Lau, *Lao Tzu: Tao Te Ching* (New York: Penguin, 1963), p. 62. All quotations from the Tao Te Ching are from this translation.
4. David Kinsley, *The Goddesses' Mirror* (Albany: State University of New York Press, 1989), p. 35. Kinsley depends on John Blofield, *Bodhisattva of Compassion: The Mystical Tradition of Kuan Yin* (Boulder, Colo.: Shambala, 1978), p. 108.
5. Laurence G. Thompson, *The Chinese Way in Religion* (Belmont, Calif.: Dickenson, 1973), p. 121.

Chapter 6: Japanese Texts

1. *Sources of Japanese Tradition*, ed. Ryusaku Tsunoda, William Theodore de Bary, and Donald Keene (New York: Columbia University Press, 1964), 1:5.
2. Ibid., pp. 25–26.
3. Ibid., p. 14.
4. Ibid., p. 27.
5. H. Byron Earhart, ed., *Religion in the Japanese Experience: Sources and Interpretations* (Belmont, Calif: Dickenson, 1974), p. 242.
6. See Ichiro Hori, *Folk Religion in Japan* (Chicago: University of Chicago Press, 1968).
7. Liza Crihfield Dalby, *Geisha* (Berkeley: University of California Press, 1983), pp. xii–xiv.